Balancing Life in Your "War Zones"

A Guide to Physical, Mental, and Spiritual Health

LeAnn Thieman

Priority Publishing
FORT COLLINS, COLORADO

Third printing 2013

ISBN 978-0-9727645-2-0
LCCN 2008921460

ATTENTION CORPORATIONS, UNIVERSITIES, COLLEGES, AND PROFESSIONAL ORGANIZATIONS: Quantity discounts are available on bulk purchases of this book for educational, gift purposes, or as premiums for increasing magazine subscriptions or renewals. Special books or book excerpts can also be created to fit specific needs. For information, please contact Priority Publishing, 6600 Thompson Drive, Fort Collins, CO 80526; (970) 223-1574; www.LeAnnThieman.com.

Contents

Prologue

How Did I Get Myself into This?

One hundred little babies lay three and four to a cardboard box, strapped in the belly of a gutted C-130 cargo jet. Bombs exploded just miles away as we raced through one hundred degree heat to save as many babies as possible before Saigon fell to the Communists.

With the first load of orphans on board, the American captain instructed us to prepare for takeoff, and I wondered how you prepare one hundred infants for this. Twenty-two cardboard boxes formed a row in the middle of the plane, and a long strap stretched from one end to the other, securing the boxes in place— a whole new definition of seatbelt safety. The sound of the motor was nearly deafening as the plane taxied down the runway. Its rumbling motion lulled the infants to near silence. We nine adults sat statue-like. Only the vengeful engine's roar broke the haunting, threatening stillness. Finally, the captain spoke: "We're out of range of the Vietcong. We're safe. We're going home!" Whoops of gladness and relief filled the plane. Immediately, we volunteers unfastened our seatbelts and hastened to tend to our charges.

Several large metal trashcans at the ends of the row held food, formula, and needed supplies. The commotion of loading babies hadn't allowed feeding time; now, all one hundred were awake and crying simultaneously. In a frantic effort to rehydrate as many as we could as fast as we could, we propped bottles on the shoulders of each baby's squalling box-mate. As the bottles emptied, I flung a diaper over my shoulder and burped one baby at a time with my right hand while bottle-feeding another with my left. My pediatric nurse experience prepared me for the infants' responses to stress, and soon the stuffy cargo compartment smelled of diarrhea and spit-up. The wee ones, once so neatly dressed in their homecoming outfits, now looked wrinkled and soiled. We volunteers were disheveled, too, but there was merriment about it all. It was joyful work escorting babies to freedom, to families.

With one in my arms and two in my lap, I shook my head in disbelief and shouted above the cacophony: "How did a mom and nurse get caught up in Operation Babylift?"

Ever since I was a little girl, I'd been drawn to the needs of orphans. At the annual church Thanksgiving clothing drives, on the podium hung a poster of a starving child…big bloated belly, big sad eyes filled with tears. It tugged my heart. So my seven brothers and sisters and I went home and tried on all our hand-me-down clothes. If something didn't fit Bob, Denny, Roger, Diane, Mary, Theresa, or Keith, I tried it on, since I was the runt of the litter. And if it didn't fit LeAnn, it went in the box for the needy. In retrospect, I think we were rather poor Iowa farm folk, but I felt rich when I could give that way.

We went trick-or-treating for UNICEF every Halloween. Our teachers gathered the whole school in the gymnasium, kinder-gartners through twelfth grade—nearly two hundred of us—and showed us film clips of Danny Kaye interacting with starving kids. Danny taught me that two and a half cents could buy a carton of milk and save a child's life. That was the first time in my life I began to believe that we *are* called to be our brother's keeper. We haven't been given everything we have in our lives to hoard, but to share.

I was still a little kid myself when I made a very important decision in my life—so important I shared it on a special day. I was only twenty when Mark and I took our romantic walk along the creek—actually, in Iowa it's called a crick. We walked on the sandbar, where my sisters and I had played, and we waded in the water, where my brothers had tormented me. And it was there Mark asked me to marry him. No sooner than I had said, "Yes!" I told him about my dream to adopt a child someday. And from that day forward it became *our* dream.

So maybe it was all these things that made me stop at a bake sale booth as I strolled the mall in Iowa City in the early 1970s. I stared into the eyes of yet another starving poster child—big bloated belly, big sad eyes filled with tears. I wanted to help, to make a difference, so I picked up some cupcakes—and some cookies—and some bread—and a brochure—and learned there was a meeting the next week. Hoping I could make a simple contribution, I attended and met a half-dozen young moms sitting around a chrome kitchen table with a dozen little kids running around. I learned about the cause, the needs of the orphans, and I signed on.

But my simple contribution grew into something more when, in a few months, the chapter president moved away. I became the chapter president. Our home became the Iowa Chapter Headquarters of Friends of Children of Vietnam. This handful of women put drop boxes in grocery stores, begged doctors' offices for medications, hosted baby showers for orphans, and coordinated lots more bake sales. We raised over five tons of supplies and sent them to Vietnam in just three years.

Attending the national conference for Friends of Children of Vietnam in Denver was a big deal for me. I'd only flown once before, and I was enthralled to meet the national officers, especially Cherie Clark, the FCVN overseas director, who had come from Vietnam. I left the conference bursting with excitement and enthusiasm for the difference we were making in orphanages there.

A few weeks later, I was completely blown away when the national headquarters called to ask me to be the next escort to bring six—key word here, "six"—babies to their adoptive homes in the United States.

I had twenty-four hours to decide whether I would go to Vietnam in April, 1975.

Chapter One

This Is the Toughest Decision of My Life!

Making Good Decisions

When I asked Mark what he thought I should do, he said what every good husband should say when posed with that question. "Do whatever you want to, honey." But I knew him. Mr. Security. Mr. Stability. Mr. Safety for his family. I knew the words "Please don't go!" were screaming inside him.

I agonized over the decision. As I tossed and turned, I saw the poster child in my head, and I wanted to say, "Yes, I'll go!" I imagined Vietnam, a destitute nation, ravaged by generations of war, and its children living in impoverished conditions. The American servicemen who'd helped tremendously in the orphanages had left two year earlier. They were sorely missed as many orphanages fell into disrepair. I grieved for the fifty thousand Amerasian children (half-American, half-Asian) left behind, knowing they would never be accepted there. Completely abandoned by society, they would never have birth certificates or legal names; therefore, they could never get a job or marry. Most Amerasian girls resorted to prostitution to support themselves and their entire ostracized families. I visualized the crippled children who received no support from the Vietnamese government, though the other orphans were allotted eleven cents per day. Everything in me wanted to go because I knew the children, the precious children, needed help and hope and health and happiness…and homes.

Though there were two dozen big reasons I wanted to say, "Yes, I'll go," there were two little reasons why I wanted to say, "No, I can't." Angela and Christie, our sweet daughters, were only two and four years old, respectively. They and their wonderful daddy were the number one priorities in my life. I'd do nothing to jeopardize that.

So, how do I decide?

I considered there had been no increase in the war in many months. Carol, the secretary of our chapter, volunteered to go with me. She called the US State Department every day, even weekends, and every day they assured her no escalation of the war was expected. We should go. We'd be safe. Mostly, though, I considered that Mark and I had taken steps to make our dream come true. We'd applied for adoption of a son through FCVN. Though we didn't expect our little boy for two years, I knew it would mean something to him someday to know his mom had been to his homeland.

So, after much thought and a whole lot of prayer, I called Denver headquarters and said, "I'll go."

And wouldn't you know it—within a few weeks there was a terrible Vietcong offensive. Every night, I sat in my living room and watched Walter Cronkite on the evening news show me pictures of the war raging closer and closer to the city I had promised to fly into.

I lost my courage.

I called the Denver headquarters and admitted my fears. They said I didn't have to go. Then I asked them who would bring out the six babies. They answered, "Probably no one."

I grieved for the lives I would mar forever if I went back on my promise.

How could something so right feel so wrong?

And why wouldn't someone ask me not to go? Then, I could find the courage—not the courage to go, but the courage to stay home.

Mom mentioned the war when we talked on the phone, but she didn't say, "Don't go."

My sisters called and said how hard the decision must be for me, but they didn't say, "Don't go."

My brother Denny took us to dinner the week before I was to leave. Surely, he would tell me to stay home. He had served in Vietnam. He had lost his right arm there. But he'd seen the plight of the children. He didn't say, "Don't go."

So how do you decide?

On Easter Sunday, the day before we were to leave, radio news reported bombing within three miles of Saigon. Our little family went to church as usual, but as the service ended, I found myself in turmoil, more uncertain than ever about what to do. Mark understood my unspoken need and signaled he'd take the girls downstairs for donuts.

If I stayed and prayed, surely God would say, "Don't go."

Alone in the empty sanctuary, embraced by the thick, sweet smell of Easter lilies, I knelt, trembling, fighting back tears. All the doubts and worries I had tried to suppress descended en masse, like a drenching rain. I felt myself crumbling. I pursed my lips together hard to keep from crying out loud, but I couldn't stop the tears trickling down my folded hands. My knees grew too weak to support me, so I sat back on the edge of the pew, put my face in my lap, and the sobs came. "What am I doing? I'm leaving everything I know and love! Please, God, give me a sign I don't have to go."

Slowly, unexpectedly, a warm feeling enveloped me, and my tears started to subside. My breathing slowed to a calmer pace. My shoulders relaxed, as an unexplainable feeling of well-being and courage filled me. I knew then, without a doubt, I was going to be okay.

I was meant to go to Vietnam.

God would take care of me.

"Thank you," was all I could manage to say; then, I left the church, my spirits soaring!

Decision made.

■ ■ ■

It's unlikely you will ever have to decide whether to fly into a warring country. Yet you're faced with decisions, big and little, every day. How do you make them?

Too often in making decisions, we don't consider what's best for us. The same qualities that call us to be caring people are those that allow us to shortchange ourselves. We cannot make good decisions when we are physically, mentally, and/or physically depleted.

Sometimes, we make decisions on the spur of the moment, in times of stress, when adrenalin is pumping. These are not the best circumstances to make any decision, big or small. You've likely been in situations like that. You're in a meeting, and somebody calls for help with a project, and they call for help, and they call for help again, and you raise your hand, and you are it, and you are in, and you are involved, and you said yes again.

That's how I, a novice, became a 4H leader of thirty kids and a hundred horses! As much as I loved it, I was in over my head with too much on my already overcrowded plate. It took me way too long to learn never to say yes at the moment. Always say,

"Let me think about it, and I'll call you tomorrow." If it is a good decision today, it will still be a good decision tomorrow.

Sometimes decisions are made too quickly in the form of misspoken words. Too often, in the heat of the moment, words are said in haste, without forethought, without peace, and lives are changed forever.

Good decisions are made in a place of peace, when one takes the time, space, and solitude to make healthy choices. Even ordinary small ones should be made in this way. Try taking deep breaths in a quiet environment to evaluate the facts before you decide. When a decision is big, maybe life-changing, get out of Dodge. Find a quiet place for an overnight stay, unaffected by the stress and turmoil. It is there, in a place of peace, that a good decision can be made.

In that quiet space, listen to your deep inner voice. You can call it intuition, conscience, the Holy Spirit, higher consciousness—whatever fits your belief system. That still, small voice is your built-in guide, your Divine guidance. It must be listened to, respected, and followed. We cannot hear it in the chaos. Be still. Listen. Follow.

Occasionally, we make decisions that are not consistent with our priorities (see chapter nine). We give lip service to one thing, claiming it is a priority in our lives, yet we make decisions that distract us from that.

Sometimes we make decisions not aligned with our values. Wouldn't the world be a better place if we all followed the Rotary Four-Way Test in our business and professional lives?

> ### Rotary International's Four-Way Test
>
> *Of the things we think, say, or do, ask the following four questions:·*
>
> - *Is it the truth?*
> - *Is it fair to all concerned?*
> - *Will it build goodwill and better friendships?*
> - *Will it be beneficial to all concerned?*

I try ("try" being the operative word here) to make my decisions based on this philosophy: *If you make the right decision today, the God you believe in takes care of the rest.* Although that is simple, it is not easy. Too often we make decisions that are not right today, but we think will be in the long run. Perhaps we twist the numbers just a bit or inflate the resume a little or step on someone on our way up, believing it will all be worth it in the long run. That never works, not in the end. What a lot of faith it takes, in ourselves and our God, to make the right decision today…based on that deep inner voice…and trust that our Creator will take care of the rest.

Early in my speaking and writing career, I won a prestigious writing contest. My prize was the honor of attending a week-long coveted writing retreat. The disappointing news was that I had a speaking engagement contracted smack dab in the middle of that week. The writing seminar was a once-in-a-lifetime opportunity, and I wanted desperately to cancel my engagement and go. But deep down in my gut, I knew it was wrong. So I missed the writing retreat and kept my commitment to my client. And from that event I got another contract worth four times my fee!

I made the right decision that day, and God took care of the rest.

This philosophy and practice takes all the pressure off. Make the moral, ethical, deep-down-in-your-gut-you-know-it's-right decision today. It's simple, and with practice, it gets easy.

That leads to the next best way to make good decisions— always tell the truth. Make sure that every word that comes out of your mouth is true. Big or small. If the project takes two weeks, don't say one. If it cost $200, don't say $190. Honesty is indeed the best policy. As a teenager, I was impressed with this quote from Will Rogers: "Tell the truth. It's a lot easier to remember."

When you decided to pursue your current path, how old were you?

Would you ask an eighteen-year-old for career advice today? Sometimes people are stuck with decisions they made before they could vote. I know an electrical engineer who, at age forty, said, "I really wanted to be an artist!" Because he chose an engineering educational path in high school, he felt "stuck" with it the rest of his life. I loved my life as a nurse and had no interest in changing careers. Yet, when my speaking "hobby" catapulted, I had to make a big decision, to do something else, to change my path and follow a new passion.

Is there something else you'll decide to be or do?

To make good decisions, there are times we need to just say, "No." This is hard for many of us to do since we think we need to be all things to all people. Dear Abby gave me great advice on that in one of her columns. I was relieved to read that I didn't have to give a reason for why I couldn't help. (I thought I had to explain that I was already chairing the church bazaar and collecting money for the cancer drive and managing thirty kids and a hundred horses and didn't have time to bake cookies for the class picnic.) Abby told me I didn't have to give a reason. All I had to do was say, "I'm sorry; I can't; I have another commitment." What a relief! That commitment can be taking care of yourself, your family, your priorities. Try it next time. It may save you from shoveling horse poop!

It's hard to say no, though, when others are pleading and counting on you, isn't it? In those situations, consider this. It's only when you step back that others can step forward.

Every time you say yes, it deprives another person of an opportunity. When you decline, it gives another a chance to serve, to learn, to grow.

If making a decision is difficult, do you postpone it for an inordinate amount of time? But not to decide is to decide. Even no decision is a decision. Think about it.

Owning a decision is key to living with it. Avoid using the words "have to." It's said we don't "have to" do anything but die and pay taxes. I'd submit that we don't "have to" pay taxes. We choose to pay them and not to go to jail. It's our choice to live in America, and paying taxes is one of the rules. Think about situations when you say "have to." Replace it with "choose to" and own your decisions and life choices. It's empowering.

Remember, where you are today is based on decisions you made in the past. Where you will be tomorrow will be based on decisions you make today. Take the time and muster the wisdom to make them good ones.

Making better decisions every day makes us better people, and as better people we are recognized and offered better opportunities, which in the end brings better rewards.

Chapter Two

How'd I End Up in a War Zone?

Coping with "War Zones" in Our Everyday Lives

On April first, 1975, April Fool's Day…now that should have been a hint…I kissed my little girls goodbye, walked out of Mark's arms, boarded a 747, and headed for Saigon. Even the journey was difficult. Carol and I got as far as Denver, where we were greeted by FCVN national officers, who gave us eighteen boxes of supplies to take along. No problem. But then they asked us the fateful question: Would we smuggle $10,000 in cash to Vietnam?

Carol, in her wisdom, shook her head no.

I listened as they explained how the Vietnamese currency had no value now and with ten thousand American dollars they could buy out a whole commissary and save the children's lives.

I shook my head yes.

I made my way to the bathroom, where I designed what I believe to be the most expensive padded bra in world history! Now, I haven't checked *The Guinness Book of World Records*. I can't seem to find that category. But I'm pretty sure I still hold that record. You've heard of Victoria's Secret? Well, this was LeAnn's secret!

We went on to California, where we were to spend the night with Carol's sister. Originally, Suzanne had been very support-ive of our going to Vietnam…until she, too, started watching Walter Cronkite. To say she withdrew her support would be an understatement. Scared to death of losing her little sister, she spent the night yelling and screaming and pleading and sham-ing us, threatening to lock us in the bathroom to keep us from going.

So, I have to admit, as our plane circled Ton Son Nhut Air-port, and I looked down at a runway lined with camouflaged fighter jets, Suzanne's words ran through my head, and the fear hit me again. *What am I doing here?*

Shaking, I descended the plane's steps and walked across that sun-baked tarmac, heading for the customs counter. I glanced down to check my chest, my heart beating heavily under all the cash. In Denver, Cheryl had told me to keep quiet and "just act natural." There was nothing natural about this. She'd also told us that we could buy anything or anyone in Vietnam, even our way through customs.

Mean looking Vietnamese guards with enormous guns glared at us. If the John Wayne World War II movies I'd seen were any indication, these were the bad guys. I shivered with fear as one waved his gun to motion me into line. I gripped the bare, grimy two-by-fours, stained by thousands of sweaty hands before us and hoped my blouse wasn't quaking with the thumping of my heart. Trembling and panting, I worried, *Will he take one look at this bodacious bosom and know this was not an act of God? Will he frisk me, find the money, throw me into prison? Will I ever see Mark and my girls again?*

"*Di chuyen!*" he barked.

I jumped.

My mind raced, grasping for something to calm me down before I gave myself away. I conjured up all the positive thinking I'd ever learned, every positive visualization I'd ever seen, every prayer I'd ever recited. Then, I remembered the relaxation breathing I'd learned in my childbirth classes. The instructor said it was a life skill, not just a labor skill.

It worked then. Will it work now?

In-two-three-four, out-two-three-four. In-two-three-four, out-two-three-four, I breathed.

Then I looked down at my huge, heaving chest and realized I was counting in one-thousand, two thousand, three thousand *dollars* and out four-thousand, five-thousand, six-thousand *dollars,* in seven thousand, eight thousand....

My own laughter released my tension but apparently annoyed the guards. I wiped the smirk off my face and with steady hands lifted my bag onto the counter. The soldier scowled and gestured to the eighteen boxes already stacked there. "What you have inside?" he demanded.

"Documents and supplies," I said as calmly as I could. He didn't seem to understand.

So I shouted, "Documents and supplies!"

Surely he could interpret the language better if I said it louder. The soldier muttered over the bags and boxes for another minute then raised his gun. I willed myself not to gasp or clutch my chest. His weapon pointed toward me...then waved me on.

I couldn't believe it.

That was it!

We were clear and out of danger...for now, at least.

Carol and I picked up our bags and headed out before the soldier could change his mind.

"LeAnn! LeAnn!" a voice called. I turned to see Cherie, the overseas director I'd met at the conference in Denver. I rushed to hug her, then stepped back and noticed her small frame looked worn and frazzled, as though she hadn't slept in days.

"Did you hear the news?" Her haggard face lit up with excitement. I realized then that we'd been traveling for over twenty-four hours and had no exposure to television, radio, or newspapers. "President Ford has okayed a giant baby lift! Instead of taking out six babies, you'll help take out three hundred if we're lucky!"

"Three hundred babies? Three hundred babies?" My mind could hardly grasp it. It was then that I knew why I had said yes, what was driving me to go. This mission was bigger than I could possibly have imagined.

Chattering with excitement, Carol and I helped Cherie pack the eighteen boxes into her Volkswagen. No, not a van. A Bug, a VW Beetle. With bags and boxes tied to the top, strapped on the back and jammed in the trunk, Carol and I crammed into the front bucket seat, and Cherie maneuvered us through the chaotic, overcrowded streets of Saigon. Two lane streets were jammed with eight lanes of traffic…hundreds of cars, thousands of bicycles and motorbikes and pushcarts loaded with people and seemingly all their possessions. Horns honked. Tires screeched. People yelled as the car veered through the congestion. Street vendors lined the sidewalks selling uncovered meats and vegetables. Smells of fresh fish and fowl permeated the hot, humid air. I winced, watching flies swarm around plucked chicken carcasses hanging from a wire rack, their heads and feet still intact.

Then, there, in the middle of the street, I saw a sandbag fortress with a Vietnamese soldier peering out the top, pointing a gun. A stark realization. *This country* is *at war.*

■　■　■

Certainly, we do not have to be in a war to be in a war zone. We all have versions of war zones in our everyday lives. What's yours?

To begin identifying your "war zones," it helps to ponder these questions:

- What are areas of conflict in your life?
- What makes you feel consistently overwhelmed and stressed?
- What things, events, or people cause you sadness and/or despair?
- What problem lurks, without an obvious solution?
- What causes you to feel incompetent and frustrated regularly?

As you examine the "war zones" facing you now and those you've endured in the past, do you often ask, as I did in Vietnam, "Why did this happen to me? And what am I supposed to learn from or do with it?"

I spent months…years…deciphering that. And I realized that coping in our "war zones" today leaves us feeling a lot like I did then.

Having too much to do and not enough time and resources to get it all done.

Being given big assignments and not enough support to get it done right.

And wanting to do it right but feeling sometimes like we're working with one hand tied behind our backs.

Giving 100 percent—some days 110 percent—but knowing it isn't enough. No matter what we do, it's never enough.

Feeling torn between work and family and volunteerism.

Having too many people all counting on us and feeling like we can't do it all.

Being so busy taking caring of everybody else that we have little time to care for ourselves.

Does some of this sound too familiar? As unlikely as it may sound, the "war zones" you are coping in are not unlike the war zones I experienced in Vietnam. Therefore, the lessons I learned there apply here today.

Do you ever feel like I did then, like you don't have enough support to do it all?

When no one asked me not to go—not my mother, my sisters, my brother, my husband, not even God—I assumed they were stifling their objections. I caution you not to make the mistake that I did. It wasn't until I spent years sorting all this out that I realized they didn't ask me not to go because, as Mark later explained, they believed in me.

They knew I could do it even when I did not.

It wasn't silent objection they felt but silent support.

I suggest that you, too, have more silent supporters in your life than you realize. Pause to consider, who are your silent supporters?

But even with support, do you sometimes feel like I did in Vietnam? Too weak, too tired, too afraid, too confused to keep it all up? To be strong enough to cope, we have to be strong physically, mentally, and spiritually and we must make good decisions to ensure that.

Sometimes we end up in our "war zones" because of our own life choices. And sometimes we wind up there through no apparent action or decision of our own. Read on to learn how to be strong and cope in your "war zones," with or without support, whether you signed up for them or not.

Chapter Three

I Didn't Sign Up for This

Sticking to Our Life Assignments

Even the deafening noises were unfamiliar to me as the thousands of Saigonese shouted to one another and bicycles and motorbikes buzzed past our overloaded VW. Men and women alike carried yokes on their shoulders with baskets or bags at both ends. I felt like I was part of a picture from *National Geographic*. Some buildings of tin and shabby wood barely seemed strong enough to stand. Others were modern and resembled those of concrete and brick in the States.

"This isn't the best part of the city. You should see the magnificent buildings and houses and beautiful beaches and palm trees," Cherie said with obvious pride. "This is like an island paradise."

We turned onto a quiet narrower side street lined with ramshackle buildings and eventually passed through the black cast-iron gates of the FCVN Orphanage Center. Palm trees and flowers surrounded the circle drive. The two-story structure, with smooth white stone and wrought-iron verandas, looked like a mansion in Europe—a bit of elegance in the midst of squalor.

Our car halted in the driveway, and immediately Vietnamese workers came to help unload the eighteen boxes.

Inside, I was thrilled to see Sister Terese, a Catholic nun I had met at the FCVN convention in Denver. Unlike the nuns I had known as a youngster, she didn't wear a habit but sported casual dress, wavy brown hair, and a lighthearted smile.

You should have seen the look on her face when I reached into my shirt and pulled out $10,000! "My mom always said I should pin some cash to my bra for emergency money when I travel," I quipped.

Everyone laughed as Cherie placed the money in the huge black safe sitting in the corner. She praised me for the risk I'd taken and told us about the lifesaving supplies she could buy.

Just then, a young man in his early twenties with unkempt curly brown hair, a bushy mustache, and sweat-stained clothes came bounding in. "Hi, I'm Ross." He pumped our hands and pushed his glasses back onto the bridge of his nose. I liked him immediately.

"Let's show you around," Cherie said as she pushed open a wooden door leading to the nursery.

Though I was a nurse working in pediatrics, nothing in my life had prepared me for what I was about to witness and be a part of. The center, which usually held ten babies, too sick to be in foster homes, now held nearly one hundred.

Several years before, all three hundred children in FCVN's care were housed in one huge three-story building. Then they had the simplest little problem…measles. Because immunizations were not available, little ones died from the contagious childhood malady. That's when the foster mother program was launched. Ads were put in local newspapers asking for breast-feeding women to love, hold, and care for babies in their homes for a small stipend. Breast milk provided the infant not only with nutrition but disease-resisting antibodies, so desperately needed. Weekly visits by a social worker and medical team made it an ideal program.

Now the babies were coming to the center by the dozens in preparation for the airlift. Every inch of nursery floor was covered with a mat, and every inch of mat was covered with a baby. Seas and seas of babbling, burping, bawling babies. Some looked beautifully healthy. Others, sickly. Nursery smells of wet and dirty diapers, spit-up, baby powder, and formula were multiplied tenfold in the hot, humid, yet meticulously clean room.

A wide open staircase took us to the next level, where the noise grew louder as dozens more babies lay closely together on bright-colored woven mats and sheets. I watched a worker slowly and tenderly feed a baby girl in an infant seat, her top lip deformed in a cleft palate. I recalled how these babies and their families were ostracized because ancient tradition suggested demons were the cause. I smiled, knowing an American family and physician could heal her.

When we went back downstairs, I gestured to a worker that I wanted to feed a baby. She nodded and handed me the one in her arms.

"Carol, take my picture," I beamed, and she took the first photo of me in Vietnam.

As I spent the rest of that day feeding, diapering, and rocking scores of babies, I knew...somehow I was on assignment.

Finally, late at night Carol and I fell into bed, exhausted.

Bam! Bam! Bam! The exploding sounds sent us upright. Fear stole my breath. "What was that?" I heard a motorcycle drive away. "Maybe just backfire from that motorbike."

Six more blasts jolted us into each other's arms.

"That's gunfire! Oh, God! It *is* the war! The city *is* being invaded!"

For the first time since I had left my little girls, the thought ravaged my mind...*I might never see my family again. I may die here.*

What should I do? I can't just sit here and wait for soldiers to come charging up the stairs.

I slithered out of bed, then crawled on my belly to the veranda. Cautiously, I peered over the railing, fearing my head could be blown off as I peeked over the ledge. The center's yard lamp lit up the street below. There was no sign of activity. Crickets chirped.

Still ducked down, I sneaked back to Carol. "Maybe soldiers are already inside. We better go downstairs and see what's going on."

We approached the steps, my mind and heart racing with fear. *What if the soldiers are in the office? What if they have Cherie? Will they take us prisoners, too? Will I ever see my family again? Maybe I should have just stayed hidden in the bedroom. That would have been pretty cowardly, though, with our fellow workers being held captive.*

We tiptoed down the steps, gripping the handrail, trying not to let our labored breaths be heard. *How can the workers sleep when the place is under Communist siege?*

Slowly, we opened the door to the office where Sister Terese sat typing. She looked up, nonchalantly. "Why aren't you asleep?"

"We heard gunshots! We thought the war was here!"

"Oh," she smiled knowingly, "they draft twelve-year-olds here. It was just the young boy-soldiers entertaining themselves during the night by shooting at rats, signs, and such."

"No Communists?"

She shook her head. "No Communists."

"Oh...never mind." With that, I went back to bed for a fitful night's sleep.

I didn't sign up for this.

■ ■ ■

I wasn't only on assignment then; I'm still on assignment. We all are.

What's yours?

Sure, you have lots of assignments in your life every day, but what is your purpose? Your mission? What is your Creator's plan for you on Earth?

To determine your assignments, begin by making a list of all the activities that consume your time. At home. At work. In the community. (It's usually better to make written lists, instead of mental lists. If you're my age, you remember George Burns and Gracie Allen, the comedy couple. Gracie was a ditz before the word was coined. She said, "I used to make mental lists, but I forgot where I put them!")

As you review your list, circle those things:

■ that you are good at

■ that you love doing

■ that make a difference.

Likely, these chores are some of your life assignments. These are areas that utilize your giftedness and fulfill you while bringing goodness to the world.

Next, examine whether your assignments are congruent with your priorities and your values. If they are not, cross them off your list.

Sometimes we deliberately and thoughtfully sign up for serving others with our jobs or volunteerism. And sometimes we don't sign up at all; a task is assigned to us, ready or not.

Which of your circled activities did you sign up for?

Which were assigned to you?

Discerning this is important, because usually it's more difficult to commit our time, energy, resources, and enthusiasm to assignments for which we did not enlist. Yet often they are duties we cannot shirk. This leads us into "war zones," where we must build strength to cope. That's the mission of this book.

I speak to thousands of caregivers every year. Many of them are paid professionals who "signed on." Millions are family members who were "assigned to." They never expected this appointment, and they many feel ill-equipped and overwhelmed.

I didn't sign up to rescue hundreds of babies in a place where gunshots woke me in the night. My devoted husband didn't sign up for what was about to befall him either. Like us, you may not see the meaning of it all while you're going through the "war zones" of your lives, but when you stay true to your assignments, you do the right thing, even though it may not be easy or even make sense at the time. You will look back and discover the purpose, the lessons…yes, even the goodness…of it all.

Chapter Four

Hurry Up in There! I Gotta Go!

Balancing Our Lives Physically

Arrangements had been made for us to dine at the American Officer's Club that night, a special treat from Cherie to us. Ross, Carol, Sister Terese, and I tried to coax her to join us, but she refused to leave her office and airlift preparations. There was no word about when we were to leave, but she wanted to be ready when it came. We felt a little guilty leaving to have fun while she continued to work.

There was a spirit of festivity in the bar, a stark wooden-paneled room filled with wooden tables and chairs. We found another American, Steve, sitting at the long table. He smiled proudly as he nodded toward his Vietnamese wife singing on the small stage at the end of the room. The pianist swayed to her emotion while accompanying her on the old upright piano as she sang a sad American melody. Her straight black hair flowed over the shoulders of her shapely body as she crooned the lonely song.

She joined us at the table and sat next to Steve, who looked like an "all-American boy" with sandy brown hair and a slim build. His light blue, deep-set eyes reflected sorrow as he told us about his plan to send his sons to his parents in the States with us on the airlift while he stayed behind to arrange passage for his wife…a difficult endeavor since she was a Vietnamese citizen.

She drank her full glass of wine quickly and returned to the stage. But the wine couldn't ease the obvious pain she felt at the prospect of saying goodbye to her little boys. Her tears flowed as she sang another melancholic tune. I thought of the pain I felt when I had said goodbye to my girls a few days earlier. I couldn't imagine the agony she felt not knowing when she'd be with her sons again.

An American dinner of baked potatoes, steak, and salad was served. Carol reminded me of the warnings others had given us en route about not eating fresh fruits and vegetables. Ross assured us, however, that all the food was brought from the United States and would be safe. I, in my usual naive trusting way, enjoyed the greens. Carol, in her usual cautious manner, declined.

Since I had eaten very little for two days, the food tasted good, and, in spite of the sadness, we talked and teased lightheartedly. Still, the cloud of worry about the approaching war cast a shadow on the fun.

"It's real close," is all Steve would say. The tortured look on his wife's face confirmed that fact. For an instant we all sat in uncomfortable, solemn silence.

Then, in an apparent attempt to change the mood, she went back on stage and bellowed out, "Won't You Come Home Bill Bailey," in her throatiest voice. We all clapped and howled. Ross put his fingers to his lips, creating a shrieking whistle.

"It's hard to believe we're in Vietnam," I shouted above the music. This was a scene out of America.

But the reality of the war returned as Ross warned, "We need to leave now if we're to get back by the ten o'clock curfew."

Abruptly, the festivities ended, and Ross drove fast through the nearly abandoned streets. "Even the toughest street boys, prostitutes, and soup vendors get off the streets an hour before deadline. They're all afraid of the Communists."

We arrived at the center to find it now filled with over one hundred babies and dozens of workers. There were only two bathrooms in the building, and I excused myself and raced to the closest one, where my abdominal cramping and explosive diarrhea began. Everyone else prepared for bed as I grew more ill. I started to dress for bed but rushed immediately back to the bathroom. It was occupied, so I ran to the one upstairs, which was also being used. The abdominal pain increased as I lay on the floor outside the door, feeling like my bowels would burst. The occupant must have heard my moaning and quickly exited. I entered the bathroom for what would be one of many times that night.

I slept fitfully on the office floor with my sweater under my head for a pillow. The increasing agony in my belly woke me, and I ran to the toilet, weak and dizzy, over and over again, scurrying quietly past the sleeping workers and babies. When both bathrooms were occupied, I collapsed on the floor outside the door. The cool tile soothed my burning face. The pains increased, like childbirth. I tried not to moan out loud as I curled in a ball, drifting in and out of sleep.

I'd never felt so physically depleted.

Will I be strong enough to carry out this assignment?

■ ■ ■

How often do you feel too exhausted to cope?

To manage it all in the "war zones" of our lives and to carry out our assignments, we have to be strong physically, mentally, and spiritually. But often, we are so busy taking care of others we don't care for ourselves. Not only do we not tend to ourselves physically, we brag about it! "I'm getting by on five hours of sleep." "I use my work-out bench as a clothes rack!" "I worked right through lunch again today!" "I didn't even stop to go to the bathroom!"

Diet

As you examine your own physical self-care, think about how often you treat yourself in ways that you would never treat anyone else. Can you imagine saying to someone you love, "You can't have anything to eat today; I'm just too busy. Well, maybe around 2:30 I'll throw you some junk food, some Fritos or something. Besides, you don't need anything to eat today; you ate way too much yesterday." You would never say that to someone you care for, but how often is that your self-talk? You know about the four basic food groups, and you can't open a newspaper without finding information about eating according to the food pyramid. But how often do you do that?

The United Nations Food and Agricultural Organization released a report in 2006 stating diet-related chronic illnesses are responsible for nearly 60 percent of all deaths. In the US, 1.3 million people die each year from self-inflicted diet-related diseases. If such a toll were inflicted by a new virus, we would mobilize all our health resources and impose a national quarantine!

It's a good idea to keep a dietary log for a week or so. I'm always surprised when I read what I've consumed, because I usually think I eat a lot better than I do. Like me, you might look back and realize that if that Wendy's hamburger didn't have lettuce on it, you didn't get any vegetables that day.

Volumes are written on healthy diets these days, but it doesn't have to be so complicated. Here is a nutshell version to get you started:

Healthy Eating, in a Nutshell

■ *6–8 servings of whole grains per day. Make sure the label says whole wheat, notrefined white flour—it's unhealthy. Rice, corn, beans, and oatmeal are good.*

■ *3–5 servings of vegetables*

■ *2–4 servings of fruit3 servings of milk products*

■ *2 servings lean meat*

■ *No transfats, no hydrogenated or partially-hydrogenated oils. (Nearly all fast foods are fried in this.)*

■ *Avoid saturated fats. Healthy no-heat oils are extra-virgin olive oil and canola. Good heating oil is extra-virgin olive oil.*

■ *Fish, shell fish, flax oil, nuts, whole grains have important Omega 3 and Omega 6.*

Not only do we forget to eat right, we forget to drink—water, that is. We've all read about the importance of drinking two quarts of water a day. How simple can that be? Yet how often do you remember to do that? Seventy-five percent of Americans are chronically dehydrated, causing daytime fatigue, memory impairment, difficulty focusing, headaches, nausea, and poor metabolism. Water regulates body temperature, carries nutrients and oxygen to cells and tissues, and flushes out toxins. Drinking five glasses of water a day decreases the risk of colon, breast, and bladder cancer.

Sleep

Do you sometimes hear yourself say, "I get by on that much sleep," or "I survive on this many hours"? Is that what you have come to? Just getting by and surviving? You would never deprive children of sleep. You know it makes them sick and grumpy. Then why do you think that doesn't apply to you?

More and more research is proving the importance of sleep. The National Sleep Foundation estimates that two out of three people are sleep deprived. We steal time from our sleep to meet increasing demands from work, travel, leisure, family, responsibilities, and social obligations. Unfortunately, our society attaches an economic and moral value on sleeping as little as possible. We even boast about it. The go-go mentality has created a 24–7 world and a nation of zombies.

The National Sleep Foundation in 2007 reported that seven out of ten Americans experience frequent sleep problems. Scientists find that when sleep is inadequate, health deteriorates, resulting in lowered glucose tolerance, impaired thyroid function, fatigue, increased heart rate, decreased strength, increased blood pressure, stomach and bowel problems, pain, and decreased abilities to fight disease.

Sleep deprivation has become a major health issue in our nation. Lack of sleep is a stressor to our bodies. It increases anxiety and decreases coping skills. Most of us will admit that we are more likely to get upset with traffic or teenagers when we are fatigued.

Lots of healing and restorative things happen in our bodies and brains when we sleep. Important hormones are released, and brain metabolism changes. Sleep deprivation increases the stress hormone cortisol while it decreases the level of two other important hormones, the human growth hormone and prolactin. These changes lead to memory impairment, poor judgment, depletion of the immune defense system, and the promotion of fat instead of muscle. (Now I've got your attention!)

> **69 percent** of all children experience sleep problems at least a few nights a week, says the National Sleep Foundation.

Grownups aren't the only ones affected by this increasing problem. A study in Japan proved that children who got fewer than ten hours of sleep a night were significantly more likely to be obese.

A recent study of over one thousand patients found that overweight people sleep less than lean ones. As we sleep, a hormone called leptin rises in our systems. Leptin controls our appetites. The higher our leptin levels, the less hungry we are. Poor sleep seems to interrupt leptin's rise, so those who don't get enough tend to be hungrier. Have you noticed that when you are over-tired, you feel more hungry? I still remember getting off 11–7 shifts feeling starved until I got some sleep.

> Although teenagers need **eight to nine hours** of sleep, only 15 percent of them actually get it, the National Sleep Foundation reported.

Sleep studies show that we experience two intervals of increased sleepiness and low performance in a twenty-four hour period. One is from midnight to six o'clock A.M., and the other from mid-afternoon to around two to four P.M. That explains why my head is nodding at the computer at that time of day. Maybe we should do as many other societies throughout the world do and take an afternoon rest and nap time. Even fifteen to twenty minutes helps. Studies show our bodies are really geared to do that, but we just ignore it.

100,000 motor vehicles accidents—that's nearly 60 percent—are related to sleepy drivers each year. 66 percent of men and 49 percent of women admit to driving while drowsy, and 23 percent say they've fallen asleep at the wheel in the past year, according to the National Highway Traffic and Safety Commission.

The National Sleep Foundation also reports that 43 percent of Americans say they are affected a few nights a week by at least one symptom of insomnia. One-third of our workers admit that lack of sleep interferes with their performance, causing decreased productivity and accidents to the cost of $150 billion dollars a year.

So what do we do about this lack in our lives? The Foundation suggests that we should budget our time to allow eight hours of sleep per night. Period. Most adults tell you they get the amount of sleep they need. They just don't need eight hours, and they're doing just fine, thank you very much. But, clearly, the research shows eight hours is truly necessary. One million Americans were studied for six years, and it was discovered that mortality rates were two and a half times higher for those who slept less than four hours.

Nearly 50 percent of men and women in America say they would go to bed earlier if they didn't watch TV or have Internet access. This seems like a perfect time to use some good decision-making skills by practicing good sleep hygiene.

For a safer, healthier life, says the Foundation, get a good night's sleep and learn to enjoy a guilt-free siesta. Tell your boss, I said so.

In kindergarten, our teacher made us lay down or put our heads on our desks and just rest for a while. I think Mrs. Geltz had something there.

For Better Sleep

■ *Keep regular bedtime hours.*

■ *Avoid alcohol and coffee later in the day. (Alcohol may help put you to sleep but actually disrupts it during the night.)*

■ *Don't eat for two hours before bedtime.*

■ *Develop stress management techniques.*

■ *Complete work early so you don't take stress to bed.*

■ *Exercise regularly but not just before sleep time.*

■ *Practice meditation and relaxation techniques.*

■ *Relax and take a warm bath before bed.*

■ *Make sure your bedroom is conducive to a good night's sleep. Keep it dark, quiet, and cool, with no pets on the bed to lick your face or take your space.*

■ *If you wake up in the middle of the night, do rhythmic breathing (chapter six).*

■ *Don't toss and turn. If you can't go back to sleep, get out of bed and go to a relaxing area to read until you become sleepy again.*

■ *Restore lost sleep as soon as possible. A power nap works wonders.*

Exercise

Regular exercise is essential to nurture our bodies physically. But that's a hard discipline for me. I don't like mundane exercise routines or gyms. I don't enjoy it, so I don't do it. That's why I appreciate the recent research by the American Heart Association proving that thirty to forty minutes of brisk walking, three or four times a week, has the same cardiovascular benefit as jogging. I imagine all the runners with the bad knees resent this information coming out now, but it sure works better for me.

Even on my busiest days, I can usually get in a thirty-minute walk. Even ten to fifteen minutes of walking or exercise is beneficial because the results are cumulative. The best way to boost metabolism is with moderate short exercises throughout the day. Taking the stairs, parking far away, and walking to the store all count.

If you're like me, it's hard in our overcrowded lives to carve out time for exercise. That's why it makes sense to try to incorporate exercise into our everyday lives. This is when I imagine my grandma looking down from heaven and laughing at us, because for all generations before us, men and women alike got their exercise from their daily activities. But now we hire people to do that stuff for us—to wash our cars and shovel our snow and rake our leaves and mow our lawns and walk our dogs—so we have time to go to the health club and work out! And when we get there, we drive around and around looking for a parking space close to the door so we don't have to walk so far to get our exercise!

When I think of all the laundry grandma did and hanging it on the clothesline and scrubbing floors and vacuuming and sweeping and gardening, no wonder she could have eggs and bacon every morning for breakfast. In our society today we have high fat and high-calorie food consumption, but we aren't hanging overalls on the line and pulling weeds and carrying bushels of garden-dug potatoes.

Small bouts of activity, even ten minutes several times a day, improves your health and probably lengthens your life, reports Gregory Florez of the American Council on Exercise. A research team led by Todd Manini of the National Institute on Aging followed 302 older adults for six years and found that **death rates went down** *as daily energy—derived from simple things like vacuuming and running errands—went up.*

The Journal of the American Medical Association reported that couch potatoes can improve their heart and lung fitness by doing everyday activities, like yard work and climbing stairs, just as much as if they went to the gym and worked up a sweat.

The US Surgeon General says exercise reduces one's risk of dying prematurely and reduces heart disease, diabetes, high blood pressure, colon cancer, depression and anxiety, and obesity. Healthier bones muscles and joints as well as improved psychological well-being are some of the other benefits regular exercisers enjoy.

Even if you don't plant an acre of garden and dig potatoes like grandma, you can get a great workout gardening and doing yard work. Squatting strengthens your leg muscles, makes your thighs fit and firm, builds your muscles in your back, and slims your waist. Spading strengthens your biceps, triceps, legs, and chest muscles. Raking works the upper back, biceps, and triceps. Pushing a loaded wheelbarrow uses almost every muscle in your body. (I'll attest to that!) Besides, fresh air is good for the lungs, heart, and spirit.

Burn 100 calories	*Burn 200 calories*
26 minutes vacuuming	*40 minutes playing badminton*
29 minutes washing windows	*30 minutes chasing toddler on beach*
18 minutes scrubbing floors	*60 minutes miniature golf*
30 minutes searching for seashells on a beach	*60 minutes dancing cheek to cheek*

A great life balance tool is to incorporate exercise into the priorities and assignments of our lives. If your partner is a priority, you can enjoy sports and outdoor activities together or go dancing…a great form of exercise, and you get to hold each other, too! If community service is an assignment, you can get good exercise cleaning a trail or lifting boxes at the food distribution center or painting a house for Habitat for Humanity. If your assignment is caring for family, you can get a lot of exercise with your kids by biking, walking, hiking, swimming, or simply playing ball in the backyard.

A report by the Center for Disease Control says

one-third

of US children are overweight. Obesity increases a child's risk of developing serious illnesses such as Type 2 diabetes.

Exercising with your children boosts their self-esteem, improves their endurance, and lays foundations for life-long fitness. You help them become more fit, and yourself, too, while building a closer relationship.

It's estimated that the average child in America spends six to eight hours a day on "screen time," such as computers, games, and the Internet. To worsen the situation, physical education classes in schools are becoming fewer and shorter. Some are even offered online. Now there's a real calorie burner!

Start a new fitness tradition with your kids. For example, reserve Sunday evenings for after dinner walks or weekend mornings for biking. You might run while your preschooler rides his tricycle or bicycle. In no time at all, these rituals will become the highlight of your week and theirs. Try this rule: For every hour of television you or your child watch, schedule an hour of physical activity.

Plan a family vacation, perhaps a camping trip or skiing holiday or canoeing adventure. In preparation, you can train and get in shape together. As a grownup, you can rediscover the joy of tag and other childhood games. You are sure to feel young again after a rousing game of duck duck goose.

According to the CDC, more than a third of young people in grades 9–12 do not regularly engage in vigorous-intensity physical activity.

At one of my seminars a young mom shared her best way of combining exercise with assignments and priorities. She said that as soon as her kids get off of the school bus, she and her husband, if he is home, too, walk around the cul-de-sac with them while they talk about their days. This ritual gives their whole family a lot more than just exercise, doesn't it? It says to the kids: You are the most important thing to me, and I can hardly wait for you get home so we can all do this together.

Exercise not only lowers your risk of heart attacks, diabetes, bone cancer, osteoporosis, arthritis, backaches, high blood pressure, depression, and stress, but it also can increase your family's health and happiness.

It's time to care for yourself as consciously as you do others—time to give your body the nutrition, sleep, and exercise it needs.

You deserve it.

Chapter Five

In All This Commotion, I Can't Hear Myself Think!

Balancing Our Lives Mentally

The next morning at breakfast, Ross and Cherie teased us about the mock invasion the night before, when I had been so sure the place was under siege. I joked along and recounted the hilarity of our actions, each time dramatizing it a bit more. I admitted my foolishness…and lingering fear.

As we ate fresh baked bread and drank cola (the only things that seemed "safe" to eat by then), Cherie gave Carol and me our assignment for the day: pack for three hundred kids.

We walked to the two-story warehouse behind the center and looked around at the rows and rows of well-organized shelves and labeled boxes. Pulling a box from a stack, I laughed. "How do we begin to find six hundred sleepers and one thousand disposable diapers?"

I pulled another labeled box from its place, brushed dust from the lid, and gasped. "Can you believe this? This is my handwriting! We sent this from my basement last month!"

The significance of the work we'd been doing in Iowa City became reality. All the efforts, all the slideshows, all the volunteer hours had been worth it.

We sorted through the shirts, pants, and playsuits we recognized, delighting in the fact that the clothes would return to the States, this time on an infant going home. For hours we worked, separating clothes by size and gathering items needed for the trip.

"They're watching *Sesame Street*," I murmured.

"What?"

"Angela and Christie are watching *Sesame Street* now. I kept my watch on Iowa time, so I know what they're doing while I'm here."

I got a little choked up as I thought of them. I missed them so much.

It was much hotter inside the metal building, and the air became polluted with mouse excrement and dirt we stirred up. By noon, the lack of an adequate breakfast took its toll, and I admitted feeling faint.

"What we need is a sugar boost." I recalled the jellybeans I had confiscated before filling Angela's and Christie's Easter baskets. Carol admitted that she, too, was not feeling well, so I made my way to the center and my flight bag to retrieve the candies. When I returned, I found Carol with her head resting on a grimy box, looking quite pale.

"Here, these will help," I said in a soothing voice as I handed her a fistful of assorted jellybeans.

Carol whined ever so slightly, "I only like orange ones."

I dropped to my knees, laughing. "You're sitting here in a war-torn country in 105 degree heat, about to faint from lack of nourishment, and you only like orange ones?"

Carol started laughing so hard, she couldn't answer. She gasped for breath and draped her body across the boxes for support. I leaned back into a pile of sorted baby clothes and rolled from side to side, howling, holding my stomach.

Gradually, we regained our composure and spent the next few hours completing that assignment. Still chuckling, we went to find Cherie, who had been to the embassy to see when we were to leave. That's when we learned. We weren't.

It seems the Vietnamese government was annoyed with FCVN for having broken a regulation the day before. We had been number one on the list to leave on Operation Babylift. But now, they not only took us off the number one position, but they also took us off the list.

When I heard that, I argued and insisted that we get our spot back. "That's not fair!" I protested. I recalled the sounds of gunfire in the night . "There must be something we can do!"

I continued arguing, begging, but my pleading was to no avail. Cherie said her hands were tied. Another organization would get the first plane.

"We still need to load just twenty babies onto the bus to take them to the Australian airliner, though," Cherie instructed. "We have a chapter and families waiting there, too."

So, with heavy hearts, in scorching heat, we loaded babies into the Volkswagen van. The middle seat had been removed, and I sat on the back bench seat. Ross handed me baby after baby, and I placed them on the seat next to me, then on mats laid on the floorboards. As they were packed in, kicking and waving their hands, one baby after another began to cry, creating a deafening cacophony.

One hour later, traffic stopped in the airport drive. In front of us, near the end of the runway, an enormous black cloud billowed into the sky.

"Dear God! What's that, Ross?"

Before he could speculate, a man in a brown safari hat and khaki clothing approached the van. He identified himself as an

Australian reporter and said, "The first plane load of orphans en route to the United States crashed just after takeoff."

Panic fluttered inside me. "No! That can't be true!"

"It's absolutely true," he insisted. "There was either a bomb on board that plane or it was shot down."

Dumbfounded, I grew angry. "This is exactly how rumors get started!" I snapped. "No one, not even in war, would deliberately bomb a plane full of babies!"

Someone hollered that the plane to Australia was ready to load, so we ended our debate. With a baby in each arm, I entered the aircraft and halted, immobilized by the sight. Hundreds of crying babies covered the floor of the plane. Canvases were stretched across parallel bars about six inches off the floor. Babies lay shoulder to shoulder on the long hammock-like rigs with a long seatbelt extended across their bodies, the entire length of the plane.

When our babies were loaded, I backed down the steps, the door slammed closed, and the plane slowly taxied away. Ross, Carol, and I started across the tarmac to the van, our eyes once again drawn to the enormous columns of smoke rising higher at the end of the runway.

As we drove away from the airport, I looked over my shoulder at the black plumes. The sound of the rescue helicopters battered overhead. I barely noticed the crowds and the noise as we drove back to the orphanage. Could the Australian reporter have been right?

The office was awash with grief. Cherie threw her arms around Ross as we entered and through her tears told us what we'd refused to believe. The first flight of orphans leaving Saigon for America, the one I had begged to be on, crashed after takeoff, killing half of the four hundred babies and volunteers on board.

The plane *had* crashed.

Then, so did I.

I slumped onto the rattan sofa, sobbing, shaking my head in my hands. I knew Mark listened to the news every morning while he shaved, and I could hear on the office radio what the news was reporting…FCVN first on the list for Operation Babylift. I couldn't call Mark and tell him I wasn't on the plane. There was no phone service out of Saigon.

"He'll think it's us!" I wailed. "I never should have come here—I never should have come here." I collapsed into Carol's arms and moaned through tears. "If they bomb one airlift plane, they'll bomb another. We might never get out of here alive."

Finally, I composed myself enough to go to Cherie, who was crying and sorting papers.

"Cherie," my voice quivered, "I'm sorry to have to say this, but I can't stay here and finish this airlift. I need to go home." I felt like a quitter and a coward.

She looked up and forced a reassuring smile. "This isn't America, LeAnn. You can't just go book a flight home. I'm afraid the only way you will get there is, eventually, on an airlift plane."

Numbly, I trudged to the nursery and robotically helped the workers feed and diaper babies, trying to fake a positiveness that evaded my breaking heart. The phone rang.

"LeAnn, it's for you," Sister said.

I almost laughed. It seemed like a joke. "Who'd call me in Saigon?"

An Associated Press reporter was on the line saying an Iowa City reporter had, incredibly, contacted him to learn whether I had been on the fatal crash. The reporter could now call Mark and tell him I was safe. The man asked whether I had any other messages for my husband.

Any messages. There was so much I wanted to say. So much he needed to know.

"Just tell him I'm okay and I love him very much," I choked.

I hung up the phone. "Oh, thank God!" Slumping onto the couch next to Carol, I sighed with relief. "My family will know I'm alive. Their not knowing was killing me inside."

Reinvigorated, I looked around at the babbling babies, took a deep breath, and almost shouted, "Let's get to work."

With renewed enthusiasm and hope, I picked up a fussing baby. My head and heart felt purged of the ruinous grief, worry, guilt, and helplessness. "It's okay, little one," I soothed. "We're going to be okay."

The tragedy only intensified the fever pitch of the airlift plans and certainly hadn't slowed the arrival of more children. Our census had doubled to two hundred. Yet, because so many foster mothers stayed and several Vietnamese nurses came to help, the infant care was outstanding.

Just very crowded and very loud.

■ ■ ■

Have you ever felt as mentally conflicted and exhausted as I did in Vietnam?

Do you ever feel so overwhelmed with a situation you wonder whether you can cope?

We are better equipped to handle our life assignments and cope in our "war zones" when we use these four mental balance tools every day to strengthen ourselves mentally.

Relaxation Breathing

Few of us need to be encouraged to be mentally active. Most of us need a nudge—or a shove—to take time every day for mental rest and relaxation. Deep relaxation breathing is one of the best and most effective tools, but it is so simple, most people discount it. It's the same breathing that's taught in yoga and childbirth classes.

The good news is, you don't have to have $10,000 in your bra to do it!

This rhythmic breathing releases not only stress and tension but endorphins, the chemical in our brain that causes us to feel good. I'm told endorphins have the same molecular makeup as morphine! We have this "drug" on tap and forget to use it by doing rhythmic breathing.

I was a childbirth educator for thirteen years, and I taught moms to breathe slowly, deeply, and easily to reduce stress in labor. The same principles apply as we "labor" through life. When laboring women get too stressed, they have increased adrenalin, and that shuts down the release of oxytocin, which makes the uterus contract and the baby come out. Too much adrenalin from increased stress makes for a longer, harder labor.

> ## Relaxation Breathing
>
> *Three or four times a day, for three to four minutes at a time, simply breathe in-2-3-4, out-2-3-4. The breaths should be slow, deep, and easy from your abdomen. Imagine a hot air balloon expanding in your chest with each breath, then deflating as you exhale. Breathe in a relaxing pace you could keep up for hours, never feeling short of breath. Breaths will grow deeper as you continue. You can add a thought with each, perhaps breathing in thinking, "I am-two-three-four" and out "relaxed-two-three-four."*

Stress raises adrenalin levels in all of us, putting us into the "fight-or-flight mode," an ancient survival mechanism left over from when cavemen were chased by wild beasts. In this mode, our bodies send all the energy and circulation to the organs needed at that moment, which takes energy away from those organs not needed for survival. That's why our hearts beat so fast and our breathing is so rapid when we get scared. We need a heartbeat and breathing to survive. What we don't need is a bladder. That's why kindergarteners wet their pants on stage. They are so nervous up there, trying to sing their songs, their little hearts and lungs work overtime to help them survive. That's why the bride has to go to the bathroom just one more time before she walks down the aisle or guys at work have to duck into the men's room before talking to the supervisor. Think of the last time you were really nervous and afraid. Did you have to go to the bathroom?

You've likely read stories of heroes in a "fight-or-flight mode" who lifted a car off an injured victim, proving that adrenalin kicks in to help the organs needed to survive. Too much adrenalin, however, interrupts healthy body function. Breathing and relaxing decreases adrenalin output and allows all of our organs and body parts to work at their best and "save" us.

A favorite couple in my childbirth class, Osvaldo and Maria from South America, taught me a lot about that. They had been to just two of my classes when Osvaldo was in a terrible car accident. When I went to visit him in intensive care, he was barely conscious but whispered to me, "The respirations, the respirations." I didn't know what he meant. I looked to make sure I wasn't standing on his oxygen tubing. Nope. So what was he trying to tell me? I went back a couple of days later when he was much improved, and he said, "LeAnn, I think that breathing you taught me in childbirth class saved my life."

He went on to explain that when he came to in the mangled car, he was afraid and in severe pain. "I was scared to death, and I could feel my heart beating too fast and the blood pumping fast from the huge gash in my leg. I knew I was bleeding to death. So I started that slow deep breathing that you taught me, and I counted in-2-3-4 and out-2-3-4, and you were right, my heart slowed down, and I could feel the gushing slow down, too." He told me how he continued that breathing when he heard the ambulance coming. "I knew it was for me, and I was scared again. And so I just kept up that breathing, and when the jaws of life ripped me from that vehicle, I just kept breathing slow. I know it saved my life."

I was walking down the hall later and met his physical therapist, who said, "Are you that nurse who taught Osvaldo how to breathe? He won't let us move him now until he does that breathing." She added, "You know, I'm having all my patients do it now, so they can relax and it doesn't hurt so much when I move them."

Osvaldo learned and then taught the physical therapist—and me—that the breathing really works. While I was having some oral surgery done, I noted that I had my fingernails embedded into the armrest. I did as Osvaldo taught me; I practiced what I preached. I started that slow, deep, easy breathing and was able to relax, and it really was much more comfortable.

A lot of activities release endorphins, not just rhythmic breathing…walking, biking, swimming, laughing, dancing, crying, jogging. Endorphins can even become addictive. Do you know runners who cannot miss a day? I have a friend who is so used to that endorphin release that if it is raining or hailing, she is inside on her bike because she can't not run. Many runners tell me that after they jog so far, they feel a surge, a second wind that pushes them on. That's the endorphins, that's the ol' morphine kicking in.

I learned a lot from my classes. One participant worked with those who are severely and mentally handicapped. He said, "Haven't you ever noticed how sometimes those individuals rock? They have the same innate survival skills that we were all born with but we just train ourselves out of. They know rhythmic rocking brings comfort."

A gerontologist piped up and concurred, "That's why old people rock. They revert back to those innate survival senses." A neonatal nurse offered, "That's why babies quit crying when you rock them."

I think we have a lot to learn from Osvaldo and crying babies.

Let's breathe slowly, deeply, and easily for three to four minutes, three to four times a day, and relax.

Robert Louis Stevenson said, "Quiet minds cannot be perplexed or frightened, but go on in fortune at their own private pace, like the ticking of a clock during a thunderstorm."

Relaxation

I told my pregnant couples that relaxation was 90 percent of a good labor, and I believe that applies to life. If moms relax between contractions, it can turn a fourteen hours labor into three hours of work. If we take opportunities to relax and rejuvenate between all those laborious times in our daily lives, that can turn a really long, difficult day into smaller, more manageable sections. We schedule so many activities into our days yet seldom schedule relaxation. Ideally, we should allocate at least thirty minutes a day for relaxation, meditation, or prayer. When we do, it becomes a habit, and we can tap into those feelings all day long.

Relaxation can be enhanced by adding music. Baroque music with the four-four beat makes our hearts beat to that time and will eventually slow to sixty beats per minute, the same as the music. Listening to it often makes the relaxation instantaneous.

Dr. Lee Berk's study at Loma Linda University proved that **music reduces stress,** *whether from illness, home, or workplace. The rhythmic beat of music releases endorphins and relieves pain.*

Pachelbel's Canon is my favorite, most effective relaxation music. I listen to it so regularly that when Mark puts the CD in while I drive, my arms and shoulders grow so heavy, I can hardly keep driving! (A little Neil Diamond perks me right back up.)

When Dr. Berk's researchers added videos blending music, scenic imagery, and positive statements, it reduced levels of hormones that suppress the immune system in research subjects. The researchers drew blood before and after the video and noted a 20 percent decrease in those hormone levels.

Keeping our bodies relaxed keeps our emotions under control. We are only as relaxed as our hands and our face are. We can't relax if we're making a fist…or clenching our teeth…or the steering wheel. It took me a long time to realize that I didn't get through the traffic jam any faster when I gritted my teeth or pounded the steering wheel. When I popped in a CD of relaxation music and did my deep breathing, I got there in the same amount of time—and in a much better mood. Isn't the road rage phenomenon unfathomable? Our whole world needs to uncurl its fist, decrease its anger, breathe deeply, and relax.

Relaxation Exercise

Sag back in your chair. Start relaxing every muscle, beginning with your toes. Stretch out your legs, flex your ankles, try to push your toes right off your feet, then let everything go limp. Let your head fall back. Roll it around so your neck muscles loosen up. Let each hand fall on your knees and rest there as limp as a wet leaf on a log. Open your eyes wide, then pretend invisible weights are attached to your eyelids, slowly pulling them shut. Imagine a soft gentle hand lightly touching your face, smoothing the tension lines away. Picture the tensions draining out of your body, leaving it calm and peaceful and relaxed.

Now see yourself alone in your favorite forest on a perfect summer's day. You are sitting with your back against a tree; you can feel the rough bark through your shirt. All around you is a forest of fir, spruce, and evergreen. The air is scented with balsam. You can hear the gentle sighing in the treetops as birds and crickets chirp. That breeze brushes against your face and cools it. In the far distance, green hills are outlined against a tranquil blue heaven. The sky is mirrored in the gleaming mountain stream gently rolling beside you, babbling along smooth, glistening rocks. The warm sun falls on your face like a benediction.

Now visualize that sun warming your body, ever so slowly from your toes toward your head. The warmth is slowly moving from your legs, over your hips, past your stomach. The warm feeling of relaxation is now entering your chest. As it does, concentrate on your breathing. Breathe in ever so slowly and breathe out. As you breathe in, you are breathing in rays of energy and comfort. Feel the warmth of these rays as they enter your lungs and radiate warmth throughout your body and relax you. As you breathe in, think slowly to yourself, "I am," and as you breath out, think, "relaxed." "I am...relaxed...I am...relaxed."

Feel that relaxation spread from your chest to your shoulders and down your arms toward your fingertips. You may feel some tingling sensations in your hands, feet, or down your spine. That's okay—it's just the discharge of nervous energy as you become more and more relaxed.

Now that total relaxation has been achieved, visualize that bright, energizing sun above your head. Feel the warmth from the rays covering and immersing your body in a blanket of warmth. The sun's rays are drawing from you all of your tensions and thoughts. The day's hassles, problems, and worries are leaving you now, and your mind is clear and at peace. Everything about you, everything around you, feels good. Your whole body from your head to your toes is now engulfed in these magical, golden rays of sun. You feel warm, soothed, and relaxed. Totally at peace and comfortable. Your breathing is slow and deep. Your face is calm and expressionless. You are relaxed. You are calm. You feel wonderful.

Look around at the sights and hear the sounds of your relaxation place. Get to know it well, for once you have created your visualization, the trip back will not be as time consuming and may become instantaneous. Take time now, to feel the sun, hear the soothing songs of the birds—the rippling stream—as you relax.

Positive Thinking

I'm a big believer in the power of positive thinking. My mentor, Dr. Norman Vincent Peale, taught me that when I read his book by that title in my twenties. He proved to me that we get what we expect in life. When we expect positive things, we act accordingly and then get positive things in return. When we expect failure, we usually fail. When we expect success, we tend to succeed. When we expect health, we make healthy choices. When we expect illness, we are often sick. Our lives move in the direction of our most dominant thoughts. We live out what we foresee. This concept is not new. Navajo Indian lore teaches

> *Perception becomes reality.*
>
> *If you perceive something... right or wrong...long enough, it becomes your reality.*

about two wolves inside us—a good wolf and a bad. Which one wins? The one that we feed.

It's said the average person has forty thousand thoughts per day, of which 80 percent are negative. Every time you have a negative thought, your brain releases negative chemicals that make your body feel bad. Think about the last time you were upset. How did your body feel? Did your heart rate increase, your jaw clench, your breathing quicken? Now, imagine one of your happiest times. When you do so, your brain releases chemicals that make your body feel good. You'll notice a slower heart beat, deeper, easier breathing, and relaxed muscles.

Dr. Peale, a pioneer in positive thinking, stated hope, faith, and truth were keys not only to happiness but to physical healing. He claimed that when you practice these virtues, you can imagine your own recovery. In his book, *Positive Imaging*, he quotes the Boston School of Medicine's study showing hopelessness—that is, the image of no recovery—actually kills. If a doctor diagnoses a fatal disease and tells the patient, and if the patient loses hope and gives up, death comes quickly. An autopsy may show the malignancy, all right, but no reason why the patient should have died so soon.

> *Kahlil Gibran wrote,*
>
> *"We choose our joys and sorrows long before we experience them."*

Conversely, Dr. Peale once knew a woman whose elderly father was hit by a taxi as he crossed the street in Manhattan and died at the age of eighty-seven. When an autopsy was performed, the doctor was amazed. "Your father had all sorts of lesions and ailments that should have caused his death twenty years ago!" he said to the woman. "Yet you say he was lively and energetic right up to the end. How do you account for that?" "I don't know," said the woman. "Unless it was his habit of saying to me every single morning, 'Today is going to be a terrific day!'" His daily imaging habit, it seemed, paid off.

In his book *Anatomy of an Illness*, Norman Cousins tells his story of being diagnosed with a fatal illness. Instead of conventional therapy, he checked himself out of the hospital and into a hotel room where he prescribed for himself laughter therapy and positive thinking for hours a day. He was so convinced that these treatments affected his health and actually cured him that he left his twenty-five-year position as an editor to take a faculty position at UCLA Medical Center. In medical research, he demonstrated that panic, depression, hate, fear, and frustration can have negative effects on human health. There is mounting scientific evidence that hope, faith, love, the will to live, purpose, laughter, and festivity can actually help control disease. These aren't just mental states but have electromechanical connections that play a large part in the working of the immune system.

Norman Cousins had blood drawn prior to doing positive visualization. He imagined a magnificent world of peace and beauty. Five minutes later, his blood was re-drawn to find he had a **200 percent increase** *in his T cells, a major immune system component.*

There is a growing field called psychoneuroimmunology with volumes of research proving that our emotions and mental states affect our health.

AIDS patients who don't deny the diagnosis but defy the fatal outcome live much longer than expected. Doctors at UCLA

George Washington University psychologist Mary Banks Gregerson, PhD, studied 119 healthy subjects who were instructed to imagine their white blood cells attacking cold and influenza cells. Researchers recorded a rise in their platelets and lymphocytes, cells that fight those illnesses.

studied whether, when people got a terrible diagnosis, it put them in a depression that inhibited their body's ability to fight the disease. They found that when people learned they had MS, AIDS, or cancer, they had an immediate downturn after they heard the diagnosis. Could their depression actually suppress their body's ability to heal?

While researchers were conducting this study at UCLA, they read in the newspaper about a ballgame at Monterrey High School where hundreds of people attended. When a few of the kids went to the first aid station complaining of feeling ill, a well-meaning school official went on the PA system and announced that everyone should avoid the vendor under the stands because of concerns of possible food poisoning. Immediately, the stadium became a sea of retching, fainting, puking people! Five ambulances transported hundreds of people to area hospitals. One hundred of them were admitted for treatment. Later that same evening, it was determined that the beverages from the suspected vendor were not the culprit. When this information reached the people admitted into the hospital, they got up, got well, and went home. Words were processed in the human mind in a way that made for illness or recovery.

This caused the UCLA researchers to ponder: If people at a ballgame can become sick enough to be hospitalized as a result of an announcement over a loudspeaker, can an announcement of MS, AIDS, or cancer have the same effect on sick people and their body's ability to cope and fight the disease?

One physician wrote in the *Western Journal of Medicine* about a conversation he overheard at breakfast between two other doctors at the American Society of Oncologists Convention. One said, "You know, Bob, I don't understand it. You and I are doing the same study, using the same application, the same entry criteria, the same procedures, the same protocol. I have a 25 percent cure rate in my study. You have a 75 percent cure rate in yours. When we are doing everything exactly the same, how do you explain it?"

Bob said, "You're right. We are doing everything the same; we are using the same drugs. We're both using Etoposide, Planitol, Oncovin, and Hydroxyurea. You call yours EPOH. I tell my patients I'm giving them HOPE."

There are about three dozen secretions in the brain. It can write one thousand different prescriptions. One is endorphins. Another, interferon, affects the immune system and fights cancer and virus cells. A third example is neuropeptides. These chemicals translate emotions into bodily events. There are neuropeptide receptors in the brain and also in the lining of the colon. That's why we have diarrhea with stress. Neuropeptide receptors are also in cells of the immune system, explaining how emotions affect our immune system.

With hope there was a 50 percent greater cure rate.

Thoughts—their thoughts—our thoughts—either build or destroy tissue.

This thinking and imaging doesn't just apply to health but everyday life.

Henry Ford said, "If you think you can or you think you can not—either way you're right."

Dr. Peale had his patients who suffered from depression picture those letters on a neon sign: D.E.P.R.E.S.S.I.O.N. Then he had them in their minds extinguish the first two and the eighth letters. Instead of depression they visualized P.R.E.S.S O.N.

Positive imagery is also effective in controlling anger. When we have a "short fuse," we can see it igniting. Then we must calmly visualize extinguishing it in our minds. Anger is one letter away from danger, and that's how it damages our health.

Bernie Siegel, in his book *Love, Medicine, and Miracles*, attests that positive thinking and visualization affect our health. Bernie, as he prefers to be called, says that he was a surgeon who simply used to remove a defective organ. But then he noticed that people who had positive thinking and visualization got better when those who did not, often did not. So he began to do research to demonstrate that what we think and visualize affects our body function.

He tells the story of a young woman diagnosed with inoperable abdominal cancer and given just six months to live. Refusing this outcome, she began to practice positive visualization every day, imagining her cancer cells as carrots and her white blood cells as rabbits. For an hour every day she visualized the rabbits eating the carrots. At the end of three months, her cancer had disappeared.

Bernie tells another story of a group of men in a chemotherapy study. Half of the four hundred men got the chemo,

> *Mayo Clinic researcher, Toshihiko Maruta, MD, proved that subjects classified as optimists thirty years earlier had half the risk of early death than those classified as pessimists or mixed. Harvard University found that men who were optimistic had less than half the incidence of heart disease and ensuing death than those viewed as pessimists. The National Institute on Aging discovered that people who reported symptoms of depression over a six-year period were almost twice as likely to get cancer as the non-depressed among them.*

and the other half got a placebo, a sugar pill. They, of course, did not know which group they were in but were told that if you get the chemotherapy, you will likely lose your hair. Of the men who got the sugar pill, 30 percent of them lost their hair!

Patients say they have less nausea and vomiting with chemotherapy when they visualize a serene white beach of Maui, cascading waterfalls, and peaceful sunsets. Apparently, that can work in reverse. One cancer patient saw her doctor in the grocery store, and it brought back such intense images of nausea with her chemo she threw up on the spot!

It took me too long to accept this truth: Our bodies and minds don't distinguish the difference between visualization and experience. They react as if they both happened.

Visualization Exercise

Close your eyes for just three minutes. Visualize yourself in your kitchen. Go to the refrigerator and open the door. Open up the vegetable bin and take out a lemon. Close the door and hold the lemon in your hand. Feel the weight of it. See the bright brilliant yellow skin. Feel the rough texture of the peel, the little nubby thing on the end. Carry the lemon over to the cutting board. Place it there and take your sharp knife and cut the lemon in half. See the lighter color. All the different divided sections. The seeds. Some seeds might even be cut in half. The juice is starting to form a little puddle. You can almost smell it from where you are. Pick up half of the lemon and bring it to your nose. Take a big whiff of that tart citrus scent. Now open your mouth and take a great big bite! Did you notice more saliva? Most people do. Here's why. Lemon juice is an acidic acid that would burn mucus membranes. So to protect us, our bodies increase the salivation to neutralize the acidic acid. Did you take in lemon juice? No. Did your body distinguish the difference between the experience and visualization? No. Based on what you were thinking and visualizing, your body responded.

An American prisoner of war was detained in a cage for six years in Vietnam. One of his methods of coping was visualizing himself playing eighteen holes of golf on his favorite golf course back home. Mercifully, he was rescued, brought home, and began to heal. On one of his very first outings, he went to that golf course and shot way under par. Why? He'd played it thousands of times. This hero proved beyond a doubt that our bodies and minds don't distinguish the difference between experience and visualization.

Have you ever awoken from a nightmare, sweating, your heart racing?

Although the scary event didn't happen to you physically, your body responded as though it had. This can work to our benefit, too. Recall your most successful moment and live it out again, visualizing it with all five senses. You can reclaim the same feelings again as your body releases the same chemicals as when you experienced it.

Positive thinking and visualization are used in sports. A basketball team was divided in half. One group shot free throws every day for an hour. The second group visualized shooting free throws an hour a day, making every one of them. At the competition, they both performed equally.

The Texas Rangers baseball team was having a losing sea-

In a Canyon Ranch Health Resort study on overweight people, exercisers were instructed to find a quiet spot, close their eyes, breathe deeply, and relax. Then they visualized each detail of their new self— how slim they looked, how their new clothes fit, how their muscles were defined. They also imagined themselves eating small portions of healthy food. Participants who did this guided imagery lost twice as much weight as those who didn't, says Michael J. Hewitt, PhD, health and healing director.

son back in the 70s, defeated nearly every game. The manager heard there was an evangelist in town, so he had the entire team wait in the dugout while he took all of the bats to the evangelist to be blessed. He came back later with blessed bats. The team went on to have a winning season and won the pennant! Were the bats blessed? It doesn't matter, does it? They believed they were, and that belief alone was what changed their actions.

I think I was born with positive genes. My mom is positive, and so was dad in many ways. Even so, I've had to work hard to stay positive in this sometimes-negative world. I still read positive thinking books, listen to CDs, and practice what I preach. I'm sure you'll agree that it's hard to stay positive when the media, coworkers, community, and family members are negative. If I hadn't been a positive thinker, I probably wouldn't have gone to Vietnam, and I probably wouldn't have survived, even en route. When we were on our way and Carol's sister yelled and screamed, blamed and shamed us, it was hard for me to take all that negativity and stay positive. That's when I remembered the words my daddy taught me, as he smiled down from heaven. "Ninety percent of the things you worry about never happen, and the other 10 percent you can't change anyhow." I paraphrase it a little, changing it to "10 percent I can handle."

> *Viktor Frankl, a Jewish psychiatrist and author, survived the concentration camp of Auschwitz. He said, "Everything can be taken from a man but one thing, the last of human freedoms—to choose one's* attitude *in any given set of circumstances."*

Mark Twain said, "I've had a lot of troubles in my life—most of which never happened."

As you begin to incorporate more positive thinking and visualization into your days, consider that the very first fifteen minutes when you're barely awake in the morning is when our brains are most receptive. This alpha state, as it is called, is when we learn a lot and have some of our best ideas. Scientists are studying this most perceptive time for our brains and exploring whether, if we have predominantly negative thoughts during this time, it may set the pace of our whole day and maybe our health and even our lives. What do you think about the first thing in the morning? Are they positive thoughts? Or grumpy mumbling? Try using that first fifteen minutes to repeat positive affirmations. Create your own list, write them down, and read and repeat them often.

Positive Affirmations

- *I am relaxed and centered.*
- *I love life.*
- *I am living my priorities every day.*
- *I am happy and blissful just being alive.*
- *I am vibrantly healthy and radiantly beautiful.*
- *I love doing my work, and I'm richly rewarded, creatively, and financially.*
- *The light of God within me is producing perfect results.*
- *I always communicate truthfully, clearly, effectively, and lovingly.*
- *I bring joy and laughter to all I do.*
- *I invest my time wisely on what's really important.*
- *My relationship with_____ is growing happier and more fulfilling every day.*
- *I have enough time, energy, wisdom, and money to accomplish my desires.*

At first, some of these affirmations are simply lies. I don't feel the least bit centered, you say. But when you repeat something over and over to yourself, your brain begins to believe it, and it starts to respond to that and cues your body to do the same. It's important to use only positive words in affirmations, because your brain doesn't hear the "no" word. For example, when I taught our son to play baseball, I reminded him to say, "I will hit the ball over the fence," not, "I won't strike out," because the brain only hears, "strike out." The other day I was carrying a cup of coffee, an armload of papers, and my car keys while trying to open the front door. (Why make two trips when you can make one difficult, time-consuming one?) In my head I was repeating, "Don't spill your coffee…. Don't spill your coffee."

You guessed it.

My brain did just what it heard.

I slopped it down my white (of course) pants.

Your brain can literally be "rewired" with positive thinking. Some neurological connections are strengthened and others are replaced. New thoughts and images stimulate new pathways in the brain and, when constantly repeated, have great impact on behavior. For example, if you constantly think, "I'm so annoyed with my husband" and think of all the irritating things he does, you are strengthening those neurological connections. Those thoughts and images become a part of your strong belief system, and that affects your mood, behavior, and relationship. If being annoyed with your husband is your objective, you will achieve it with this mental training. If growing your loving relationship is your goal, you need to change your mental engineering, using positive thoughts and images. Make lists of all you love about him—long lists—and review and repeat them often. Soon your brain will be rewired, and your thoughts, images, and actions will change. The more you repeat, "I love my man!" the greater the neurological impact.

As you're implementing positive visualization to actualize your goals, remember to appreciate what you have along the way. One woman visualizing a Corvette convertible

If you find yourself mentally repeating negative thoughts about a person or situation, write them down as they occur throughout the day. Writing them releases negative emotions and makes way for a new script. After three or four days, target the most frequent or disruptive thoughts to rewrite. For example, one working mom found herself writing, "I'm the first one up in the morning and the last one to sleep at night, and nobody appreciates all I do." Then she rewrote it as, "I love my family, and I choose to show that love in all I do for them." Soon, her attitude changed, as did her actions, and, consequently, her family's.

complained negatively every day about her rusty old van. Be grateful that you have a car as you visualize a better one.

Positive thinking and imaging are powerful and mysterious forces in human nature, capable of bringing about dramatic improvements in our lives. Einstein said, "Imagination is more powerful than knowledge." It's a kind of mental engineering. Your mind is a computer, and you have sovereign control over the input.

How are you going to incorporate positive thinking and visualization to change your life?

Laughter

Our third mental balance tool is the "funnest"…laughter. Statistics show that little kids laugh about four hundred times a day. One study showed that grownups laugh only eleven, and yet another said only four…and you know some people who can't meet that quota!

Proverbs tells us, "Laughter is good medicine, but a broken spirit dries the bones." Did you know there is medical evidence to corroborate that theory? Volumes are written today on the therapeutic benefits of laughter. Because it is a rhythmic activity, it is a great endorphin releaser, too. When Norman Cousins checked himself out of the hospital and into a hotel for self-prescribed laughter therapy, he found that ten minutes of belly laughing provided two hours of pain relief.

According to the Association of Applied and Therapeutic Humor, an organization of six hundred doctors and healthcare professionals, science has proven that laughter kills tumor cells and fights diseases. They would like to see laughter become part of patients' written prescriptions. If a medicine had great physiological, psychological, and immunological effects, the FDA would be on it like crazy, regulating it and running trials on it. You wouldn't be able to get it for ten years. What's nice about human laughter is that it is free and has no side effects.

Dr. William Fry of Stanford University Medical School likened laughter to a form of physical exercise. It's like jogging on the inside. It lowers your blood pressure and heart rate, improves lung capacity, massages internal organs, increases memory and alertness, reduces pain, improves digestion, and lowers the stress hormones, cortisol, and adrenalin. It's good for the muscles involved in laughter, your chest, and abdomen, and it exercises those muscles not involved. Dr. Fry said laughing 100–200 times per day is the cardiovascular equivalent of rowing for ten minutes. I don't know about you, but I'd much rather laugh than row.

In addition to physical benefits, laughter also has psychological benefits. It teaches us to be out of control, brings us into the moment, helps us transcend our problems, brings us closer to people, and helps us think more clearly.

One of the biggest reasons grownups don't laugh more is fear of looking foolish. It's a primary fear. We are more afraid of looking foolish in public than of a nuclear attack, which came in second on surveys. What's wrong with this picture?

One reason we don't laugh more often is because we've been conditioned not to. What did you hear as a child? "Wipe that smile off your face." "This is no laughing matter." "Is everything funny to you?" "You're making a fool out of yourself." "Grow up. Act your age."

We don't stop laughing when we grow old; we grow old when we stop laughing.

We need not only to allow ourselves to laugh often and freely, but we also need to create occasions to do so. Laugh at yourself…you're your own best material.

After Norman cured himself with self-prescribed laughter therapy, he did a study with two groups of people with pain. Half of them got a pain pill; the other half got placebos. The half that got the placebos picked their own laughter therapy and did it for two hours every day. The results? The patients who had laughter therapy and the placebo had the same degree of pain control as those who took drugs.

Funny things are all around us, too; we just need to be more in tune to find them. These old favorites still make me laugh!

■ *Instructions on Dentyne gum…put one or two pieces in mouth and chew.*

■ *Fritos…you could be a winner, no purchase necessary, details inside.*

■ *Swanson frozen desserts…serving suggestion, defrost.*

■ *Bread pudding…product will be hot after heating.*

■ *An iron…do not iron clothes on body.*

■ *Children's cough medicine…do not drive a car or operate machinery after taking this medication. (I'm sure we could reduce the rate of construction accidents if we got those two-year-olds with colds off heavy equipment.)*

■ *Nytol sleeping aid…warning may cause drowsiness.*

■ *Dashboard windshield sun protector…do not drive with sun protector in place.*

Newspaper headlines are another great source of humor. These made me spew my breakfast cereal:

- *Diaper Market Bottoms Out.*
- *Antique Stripper to Display Wares at Store.*
- *Lawyers Give Poor Legal Advice.*
- *Twenty Year Friendship Ends at Altar.*
- *Queen Mary Having Bottom Scraped.*

If we don't find enough to laugh about in our lives, we must create it.

Creating Laughter in Your Life

- *Make a list of things that make you laugh, and add them to your everyday life.*
- *Record, replay, and rent funny movies, shows, cartoons, bloopers, and watch them often.*
- *Listen often to the comedian who makes you laugh until you wet your pants.*
- *Plan a regularly scheduled comedy night.*
- *Tough times at work and home? Each day, put a piece of tape on your sleeve indicating where you've had it up to.*
- *Throw a party funded by money put into the laughter pot every time someone is caught being grumpy.*
- *Write FUN on the top of every meeting's agenda and start with something funny.*
- *Surround yourself with funny pictures of you, friends, and family.*
- *Create a laughter bulletin board at work and home where everyone contributes cartoons, baby pictures, etc.*
- *Challenge others to have a best joke contest.*
- *Buy funny greeting cards. Stop while you shop and read a few.*
- *Listen to kids laugh. It's contagious.*

I met a native of India who confirmed what I'd once heard, that every morning the elders gather in the park there to laugh. They do, he said, for the therapeutic effect of having a group of people chanting "Ha, ha, ha" together. Soon, they are all laughing naturally, and whether they call them endorphins or not, what they do know is that it is very healing.

Try it sometime soon. Get a group of people together and have everyone say, "Ha, ha, ha, ha," over and over. (This is where the number one fear of feeling foolish kicks in.) Next, add knee-slapping, then foot-stomping to the "Ha, ha, ha" chant, and before you know it, the whole bunch is rollicking in laughter! And laughing together creates a special bond.

Yes, even fake laughter is healing. Smiling muscles trigger the hypothalamus to tell the body to tell the brain, and it releases endorphins. Slapping the knees and stomping feet add to it. The fact that your chest feels lighter and your heart is not so heavy is no coincidence. Healing has occurred.

"Humour is an essential part of psychotherapy treatment that we give heart patients. We advocate that five minutes of laughter is good enough to rejuvenate the body for twelve hours," says Dr. S.P. Bijotra, vice chairperson, Department of Medicine, Sir Ganga Ram Hospital in New Delhi.

"Humour therapy is used extensively in yoga and other alternative therapies. Joggers laughing heartily in parks most early mornings is a common sight."

As a child, did you ever gather your friends and play the game where you lay on the floor with your heads on each other's tummies? The first person starts to laugh, and before you know it, the laughter goes around the circle and the whole bunch is in hysterics, giving a whole new meaning to "belly laugh."

Let's reclaim the laughter of our youth. It's is a gift to ourselves and to those around us.

Forgiveness

This fourth and final mental balance tool may be the hardest. Yet we waste a lot of our energy, our health, and even our lives when we fail to forgive.

Buddha, Jesus, and other spiritual figures taught this holy philosophy. It's not only good for our souls but for our hearts and bodies.

So, starting today, we forgive, first of all, ourselves. For any past mistakes or indiscretions, we forgive. What we did back then was who we were then, based on what we knew then. It has nothing to do with who we choose to be today.

And starting today, we forgive somebody else, no matter how horrific the offense.

And I know: Some are horrific.

It took me too long to realize that when we refuse to forgive someone, it doesn't hurt them, it only hurts us. Why would we give someone who wounded us so deeply the power to continue to harm us with sleepless nights, upset stomachs, and headaches?

> *Forgiveness training can provide specific improvement in physical well-being, reports Frederic Luskin, MD, PhD, at the Stanford Center for Research in Disease Prevention and director of the Stanford Forgiveness Project. The treated group showed significant decreases in symptoms such as chest pain, back pain, nausea, headaches, sleep problems, and loss of appetite.*

I know people who are mad at people who don't even know they're mad at them.

I know people who are mad at dead people.

We must forgive. It is freeing and healing.

Organized religion and twelve-step programs have long recognized the healing power of forgiveness. It has helped people break through intergenerational cycles of revenge, anger, and bitterness and resolve resentment within relationships.

Steps to Forgiveness

First, realize you have been unjustly treated and have a right to be angry.

Second, decide that forgiveness is an option of choice. A positive decision. Forgiving does not equal forgetting, and sometimes there is no reconciliation. A widely accepted definition of forgiveness is to pardon, to release from further punishment.

Third, reframe the offender. Acknowledging how they were raised and treated helps reveal how they were probably victims of similar treatment—although that does not mean condoning or excusing such behavior.

Fourth stage occurs when you begin to develop feelings of empathy or even compassion for the offender. Not because of what they did, but in spite of it. Finally, you can forgive, often breaking the cycle and putting to rest feelings of revenge, anger, and guilt.

Positive visualization is an effective forgiveness tool. Visualizing a quarrel ended, a relationship restored, the pain and alienation eliminated is a tremendous first step. Sometimes you can confront the offender directly, but sometimes that is not possible or advisable. Then it may help to imagine vividly the face of the person who has wronged you and to say out loud, "I forgive you." Writing a letter, whether you send it or not, releasing the other person…and you…can promote the healing.

Equally important is to accept forgiveness. It's an antidote for poisons that can corrupt the body and damage the soul.

Forgiveness sometimes feels like a short-term loss for a real long-term gain. Some confuse it with a weakness, but it demands great spiritual strength and moral courage, both in granting and accepting it. So write the letter, make the call, or say it face to face— whatever it takes, just let it go —move on.

Mark Twain wrote, "Forgiveness is the fragrance a violet sheds on the heel that crushes it."

Forgiveness is an empowering choice. Sometimes forgiving other people is the greatest gift we can give ourselves.

Those who fail to forgive have increased cardiovascular disease and lower immune-system function, says Everett Worthington, Jr., professor at Virginia Commonwealth University. Forgiving people have lower divorce rates, less clinical depression, and better social support.

These four mental balance tools are simple—though not always easy. How are you going to incorporate them into your life every day to increase not only your happiness but your health?

Chapter Six

So, Help Me, God!

Balancing Our Lives Spiritually

The walls and floors seemed to vibrate with the sounds of crying and chattering.

"We'll be working into the night," Cherie said as she plopped a stack of files onto the table. "Remember I told you how the Vietnamese government wouldn't allow Amerasian babies to have registered legal names or birth certificates?"

I wiped a baby's bottom and tucked the diaper beneath it. "I remember."

"Well, they just made a new rule. Every baby leaving on Operation Babylift has to have a legal name and birth certificate."

"What?" Ross asked incredulously.

"How are we going to manage that?" I wondered out loud.

Cherie nodded to the adjoining room where a man in a white lab coat worked intently over a child. "Dr. Cuong is here, as he is almost every night. He's going to do physicals on all the babies and estimate how old they are. We, then, will assign them birth dates and make up proof-of-birth-statements, which the government says they'll accept."

She pulled hospital ID bracelets from one of the eighteen boxes we'd delivered and tossed them to Ross. Then she handed

Sister Terese a Vietnamese name book and said, "By morning, every baby will have a certificate and a legal name."

Dr. Cuong joined us and began to tenderly examine another baby. As he provided information, we provided a name, and Sister Terese typed it on the ID bracelet.

"Hey, this is Jeni," Ross said of a cutie in his arms. "That's all we've ever called her."

"'Jeni' ain't gonna cut it getting her out of the country," Sister teased as she looked in her book of names.

"Is this legal?" Carol couldn't help but ask.

"We didn't make up the rules; they did," Cherie said. "We just have to find a way to comply."

Sister Terese continued to page feverishly through her book, and chuckles turned to laughter as Ross began concocting silly, rhyming names. It felt good to laugh again.

At 3:00 A.M. Carol stretched out on the rattan couch, and I curled up on the floor of the office. A few hours later I awoke to sunshine in my eyes, and I squinted, expecting to see the Madonna and Child picture on my bedroom wall at home. Instead, a gecko stared at me, reminding me where I was.

I sauntered to the kitchen for my usual cola and French bread breakfast.

Cherie and Ross greeted me with particularly bright smiles. This is when Cherie often gave us our assignments for the day, but I was totally unprepared for this one.

She broke a piece of soft bread from the loaf. "LeAnn, you and Mark will be adopting one of those babies in the next room."

I sat stunned. In all the commotion, I hadn't considered that our two-year wait for a child would be dramatically shortened now. Before I could comprehend her point, she went on. "You can wait to be assigned a son from across a desk in Denver…."

She paused to touch my hand. "Or you can go in there and choose a son."

Speechless and dazed, I felt my heart racing with excitement, then fear.

"Really?" I finally croaked. Surely, I had heard her wrong.

Cherie's tired eyes danced. "Really."

"So I can just go in there and pick out a son?" I could feel my heart beating in my neck.

Carol and Ross snickered at my inability to comprehend the message. Cherie nodded again.

I turned to Carol. "Come with me."

She jumped up immediately, and we approached the door to the nursery together.

I paused and took a deep breath. "This is like a fantasy. A dream come true."

One of the last things I had told Angela and Christie was that our baby wasn't ready yet and wouldn't be coming home with me. Now, in this world of incredible events, something even more incredible was about to happen.

Expectantly, I pushed open the door. Babies on blankets and mats, in boxes and baskets and bassinets and cribs.

"Carol, how will I ever choose? There are over one hundred babies here now."

"Some are girls," she offered. "That'll limit your choices a little."

I almost laughed. "I've heard of exciting shopping sprees before, but this is ridiculous! I wish Mark were here."

One baby in a white T-shirt and diaper looked at me with bright eyes. I sat cross-legged on the floor with him on my lap. He seemed to be about nine months old and responded to my words with cute facial expressions and animation. I noticed he had a second bracelet on his ankle, with a family name on it. He had already been assigned.

Another child caught my eye as he pulled himself to his feet beside a wooden crib. We watched with amusement as he tugged at the toes of the baby sleeping inside. His eyes met mine, then he dropped to his hands and knees and began crawling to me. I met him halfway across the room and picked him up. He wore only a diaper, and his soft, round tummy bulged over its rim. He smiled brightly at me, revealing chubby cheeks and deep dimples. As I hugged him, he nestled his head into my shoulder.

"Maybe you'll be our son," I whispered. He pulled back, staring into my eyes, still smiling. I carried him around the room, looking at every infant, touching one, talking to another. The baby in my arms babbled, smiled, and continued to cuddle. I couldn't bring myself to put him down as we went upstairs where the floor was carpeted with even more babies. The hallway was like a megaphone.

"Let me hold him," Carol coaxed, "while you look at the others."

I wove my way to the blanket at the end of the room and sat caressing the infants there. As I cradled one in my arms, I could feel the bones of his spine press against my skin. Another's eyes looked glazed and motionless. Sorrow gripped me.

The little boy Carol was carrying for me patted my shoulder. As I turned to look, he reached his chubby arms out to me. Taking him from her, I snuggled him close.

Someone had loved him very much.

Downstairs, we meandered from mat to crib, looking at all the infants again. I wished I could adopt them all. But I knew there were long waiting lists at the Denver headquarters of hundreds of families who had completed the tedious, time-consuming application process. Each of these precious orphans would have immediate homes, carefully selected for them.

"How do I choose?" I asked myself as much as Carol. Recalling our chosen name, I muttered, "Which one is our Mitch?"

The baby boy in my arms answered by patting my face.

I sat on the floor, slowly rocking him back and forth in my arms. I whispered a prayer for the decision I was about to make. "Help me, God," I prayed. "Show me, Lord, that this decision is right."

The baby snuggled into the hollow of my neck. I could feel his shallow breath and tender skin as he embraced my neck and my heart.

I recalled all the data we had collected, all the letters of references from friends, bankers, and employers, all the interviews with the social workers.

It had all been worth it for this moment.

We rocked in silence, clinging to each other. Then, with tears in my eyes and immense joy in my heart, I walked back through the nursery door to the office. "Meet our son, Mitchell Thieman," I announced, hardly believing my own words.

Ross, Sister, and Cherie gathered around and hugged us. Cherie brought a name tag, and I eagerly scrawled "Reserve for Mark Thieman" on it and placed it on Mitchell's ankle. Joyful tears streamed down my cheeks. For a moment all my fears were gone. I no longer wondered why I had been driven to make this journey. "This is why God sent me to Vietnam," I whispered.

I had been sent to choose our son.

■   ■   ■

Are there days when you wonder, *Are you there, God?*

Are there times you feel the Divine presence and guidance in your life and other times when you wonder how it got so far away?

On those days, remember—it wasn't God that moved.

Creating a spiritual balance to our lives is as crucial as the mental and physical, for we cannot cope in our war zones without it.

Gallup polls say that 94 percent of Americans believe in God. Therefore, I call on you to be in touch with the God you believe in every single day. We can't just wait for weekends.

Even if it is just for fifteen minutes, take time for prayer, meditation, or reflection. "Fifteen minutes?" you say. "I barely have time to eat, sleep, and exercise. So where in the heck am I supposed to come up with another fifteen minutes for spiritual time?"

This was a hard discipline for me. I knew it was important, but I just couldn't seem to allocate the time. Instead, it seemed I just yammered on and on to God all day long, which I think is important, too, but I was ignoring the need for quiet.

As I was grappling with this, I happened to talk to a friend who was telling me, in idle conversation, about his busy week. He had worked over sixty hours, driven sixty miles to Denver several times, harvested his garden, and even visited a friend's brother in jail. Then he casually mentioned something that came to him during his hour of prayer that morning. I said, "Bob, I can barely find time for fifteen minutes; how do you do an hour?"

Then he said the words that still echo in my head every day. "If I didn't start my day that way, I would never have time for the rest."

Determined to incorporate that same, though significantly less time-consuming discipline, I bought a little daily reading book, thinking that would be a great way to start. But being the task-oriented, productive nurse that I am, I couldn't sit down and read it—no, but I could read it every day while I dried my hair. So each morning I flattened the booklet on my bathroom counter and read it out loud as the hairdryer buzzed and blew. Then, a few weeks into this routine, it occurred to me: "You know, LeAnn, I think you're supposed to sit down…shut up…and listen."

Listen.

To that deep inner voice.

You can call it intuition, the Holy Spirit, gut feeling… whatever fits your spiritual belief system.

Few of us see burning bushes or hear the actual voice of God, but we all have the inner voice, which is the Divine guidance for our lives, and we cannot hear it in the chaos.

With this revelation, I started setting my alarm fifteen minutes earlier. Goodness, you'd have thought I'd set it for 3:00 A.M., the way I moaned and groaned as I hauled my lazy self out of bed! To my surprise, however, I learned that the days I didn't start that way were ones that didn't go so well; I was far less productive and happy. I soon learned that fifteen minutes was a great investment.

One night on the evening news I saw Dan Rather interviewing Mother Teresa. He asked, "What do you say when you pray?"

She said, "Nothing. I just listen."

Dan queried, "What does God say?"

She answered, "Nothing. He just listens."

In that listening-silence is the wisdom, the guidance, the direction we can only "hear" in the peace and quiet.

A twenty-eight year study of 5,200 men and women, including Jews, Muslims, Buddhists, and a broad variety of Christian denominations, plus atheists and agnostics, found frequent service attendees had healthier lifestyles. They were more likely to quit smoking, increase exercising, reduce weight, be less depressed, stay married, and have one-third reduction in mortality, concludes William Strawbridge, PhD, at the Human Population Lab of California's Department of Health Services.

People who attend church, temple, or mosque regularly have half the levels of the blood protein interleukin-6, which, in high levels, is associated with AIDS, cancer, osteoporosis, diabetes, and Alzheimer's. Patients affiliated with a religious community had 50 percent shorter hospital stays than those with no religious affiliation, reports Harold Koenig, MD, director of Duke University's Center for the Study of Religion, Spirituality, and Health.

Modern medicine is finally learning that we are not just physical beings but spiritual beings as well, and the spirit has great influence on healing.

Duke University found that people who attend church are healthier and less depressed. Interesting in this study, though, was the finding that people who stay home and watch evangelists on television are more depressed! So there must be something with attendance, the camaraderie, the unity found there.

Researchers conclude that churchgoers have meaning in their lives, a better sense of control, and they can relate better to other people. These all have positive health benefits.

Half of America's medical schools now teach courses in religion and spirituality because of their impact on patients' health. Ninety-nine percent of doctors believe there is an important relationship between the spirit and the flesh, according to the Associated Press.

Harvard's Mind/Body Institute agrees that prayer and religious ritual can relieve stress. Herbert Benson, M.D., found that praying ten to twenty minutes a day can decrease blood pressure, heart rate, breathing, and metabolic rates.

Believing and trusting in a Higher Power takes most of the stress off in life. When you know it is not all up to you, that God has a plan and you trust that, all you have to do is your very best, and then let go.

Let go and let God.

I only know one scripture reading by heart. I'm not proud of that; it's just the truth. Every morning, without exception, I say these words from the 25th Psalm: "Show me your way, oh, Lord. Teach me your path. Lead me in Your truth and teach me." I change the next line by adding my own, "…because I don't know what the heck I'm doing."

But God does.

Trusting that takes away the worry.

Surely you, too, can find ten to twenty minutes a day for spiritual balance, so it becomes a habit, a daily coping tool. This helps build a spiritual reserve. With it, you can keep a balance on the spiritual tightrope…then, when something shakes the rope, you won't lose your grip.

You'll have the Power and Strength to hold on.

Consider joining the 90 percent of Americans who pray. Boost the 40 percent who go to church weekly.

So often we choose a way of life that best suits our bodies…let's decide on one that also nurtures our souls.

> *Patients who were prayed for but didn't know it had fewer life-threatening complications and needed less medication, said a study by cardiologist Dr. Randolph Byrd at San Francisco Medical Center, a decade ago. Dr. Byrd's findings have been duplicated in a study of 990 cardiac patients led by Drs. James Vacek and William Harris at St. Luke's Heart Institute in Kansas City, Missouri. "There is now convincing data that people who have strong spiritual beliefs do better, even in serious illness," says Dr. Vacek.*

10 Ways to Pray, Meditate, Reflect...and Listen

1) Set aside time, even fifteen minutes, to be alone and quiet. Relax your mind and body. Breathe. Hush your heart. Bid all your senses be still. Listen. In the silence, you will get a sense, a feeling, an intuition that will guide you. Respect and follow that.

2) Talk to God in a simple manner, yammering on about what is on your mind. Formal language and prayer...even words...are not necessary. God will understand you.

3) Utilize your positive thinking and affirmations. Repeat, "I believe I am always divinely guided. I believe I will make the right choices. I believe God will make the way."

4) Utilize your positive visualization. Imagine a blackboard with jumbled words, phrases, and wrong answers—in short, a sorry record of mistakes. Then imagine the Creator sweeping a sponge across it, wiping it clean. Release the guilt. God forgave you. Forgive yourself. It's as simple as that.

5) Repeat, "With God's help, I now forgive." Anger, resentment, and hatred set up barriers that deprive us of spiritual power. Let go and let God do the judging and punishing.

6) Surrender a problem. Trust a Larger Force at work, healing you and solving your difficulties.

7) Utilize prayer minutes. Talk to God throughout the day, on the subway, at your desk, while folding laundry. Close your eyes and have a word or two with God. Feel your Creator's presence. Can't close your eyes? (Not a good idea on the Interstate.) Use that time to talk to God anyway.

8) Make family prayer time. Perhaps a short prayer with the meal or before bed. Light a candle. Set aside a sacred time.

9) Practice thanksgiving. Be less concerned about what you lack and more grateful for all you have.

10) Join a faith community. Study holy works. Read inspirational writings. Surround yourself with faith-filled people and places.

Chapter Seven

I Want My "Juice!"

Asking for What We Need to Put Lives in Better Balance

"We're outta here!" Ross nearly leapt into the room. "We leave this afternoon!" He motioned to the babies on the floors, in infant seats, clothes baskets, cribs, and boxes.

"Pack up!" he ordered with a laugh.

Workers in every room began dressing the babies for their homecomings. Infants were changed from their daily attire of diapers and sleepers into their Sunday best. I beamed like a proud mama to see them in shorts, shirts, and ruffled dresses we had shipped from Iowa. Now the clothes were going back to the States…on a baby…going home.

The women, who had previously diapered and fed them so merrily, now openly cried as they dressed them one last time. Many of the foster mothers who had come to help wept as they prepared to relinquish the baby they had cared for as their own. We hugged them, barely able to imagine their feelings. "We're so happy for them," one said in tearful, broken English.

In the kitchen, workers prepared hundreds of glass bottles of formula. When I noticed each was boiling hot, I cautioned the woman at the stove. In choppy English she reported that it had been done deliberately, figuring the formula would cool and be just the right temperature by the time we boarded the plane. She smiled proudly at what she thought was an ingenious idea.

I hoped she was right.

The city bus that was to transport the babies to the airport was too large to maneuver the narrow streets near the center, so it parked blocks away on the main street. First, we loaded the babies into a Volkswagen van to take them to the bus. The center seat was removed, and I sat on the back bench seat. Twenty-two babies were placed all around me on the seat and floor, as we had done for the trip to the Australian flight.

That was before the crash.

My heart jolted with fear, and I gripped the baby in my arms. Would our flight be bombed or sabotaged, too? My worry was interrupted by the sounds of more babies crying and the pressures of the task at hand.

Ross slowly snaked the van to the waiting city bus. The infants were too crowded to roll around as the van crept through the narrow street. We carried the wee ones onto the big bus and placed them three on a seat...or four if they were little. Then the van returned to the center for more.

After four trips, the city bus was full to capacity. Once we got this first bus of one hundred delivered to the airport, we'd return for the second hundred...and Mitch. I had hugged him and kissed his chin and cheeks, explaining that he'd be on the next load and we would leave for home together. Home. I grinned, imagining us there with his daddy and sisters.

Now, every baby on every seat of the city bus was bawling. We had placed their heads against the seat backs to prevent them from rolling forward when the bus slowed or stopped. The task of transporting them safely seemed monumental.

Carol, Ross, and I placed ourselves in the aisles to watch over them as the bus slowly inched its way to the airport. The motion of the bus and the hum of the motor soothed some of the infants, but the three of us still had to shout to be heard above the wailing. We stretched our arms and legs to guard the babies from falling, and we laughed as we looked at one another balancing spread eagle, trying to steady the precious cargo.

"I think I saw this on *I Love Lucy* once!" I shouted.

Carol and Ross laughed in spite of the stress.

I knew, certainly, that there was no time to make better accommodations for transportation. Vietnam's President Thieu had set a time and date for our departure, and it was FCVN's problem to meet that deadline. His seemingly deliberate efforts to make the airlift fail only served to strengthen our conviction to make it succeed.

There were a few older children on board, and they tended to the babies placed beside them. A little girl with straight black hair patted the backs of the three babies next to her as she cooed to them in Vietnamese. I listened as another boy sang native songs while rocking the baby whimpering in his arms. The bus driver turned the corners at a snail's pace, and we moved from seat to seat, patting, soothing, stabilizing squalling babies.

They each looked so cute in their frills and fancy clothes, but their little arms and legs flailed as they screamed simultaneously. Four toddlers, probably only two or three years old, sat together on the last seat of the bus. As their sweaty little bodies jostled in the sweltering heat, they gazed at all the bawling babies, and one by one they joined in the chorus of tears.

"Juice!" one pleaded. "Juice!"

■ ■ ■

Do you ask for your "juice" when you need it?

As grownups, we tend not to do that. First of all, it takes us way too long to figure out it's "juice" we need, and then if we do figure it out, we tend not to ask for it. Instead, we internally whine, "I didn't get juice today. I hardly ever get juice anymore. Nobody seems to care if I get my juice or I don't!"

Ask for your "juice" lovingly—from yourself, your family, your coworker—to put your life in better balance, physically, mentally, and spiritually.

Science is proving more and more the critical connection between body, mind, and spirit. It has been irrevocably proven that anxiety, alienation, and hopelessness are not just mental states. Neither are love, serenity, and optimism. All are physiological states that affect our health, just as clearly as obesity or physical fitness. The challenge is to nurture each system...mind, body, and spirit... to sustain and heal the other.

Relaxation

with yoga, prayer, or simple deep-breathing exercises, can help counter the effects of chronic stress and improve our health, reports Dr. Herbert Benson of the Mind/Body Medical Institute in Boston.

On one hand, it might seem a little discouraging to think that physical pain and disease cannot be confined to our bodies but spread to our emotional and mental outlook, but, on the other hand, it's encouraging to know that, because the physical, mental, and spiritual are interrelated, we can call upon all three to find healing in times of brokenness.

As we try to balance our lives better in these three ways, it often helps to combine the three. Some people enjoy prayer-walking. Some listen to motivational tapes while exercising, combining the physical and mental. Others listen to religious music or spiritual CDs when they work out.

On the too-rare occasions that I clean my house, I like to do it to the old time rock 'n' roll—you know, the kind of music that moves your soul. I reminisce about the days of old while I vacuum my house in record time, getting great exercise while clearing and delighting my mind.

I sing entire show tunes when I drive in my car. Singing is great for my lungs and a great endorphin releaser for my mind. When I get to a stop sign, singing the soundtrack from *Camelot* at the top of lungs, I look around and notice everybody around me is laughing. So I figure it is a good endorphin releaser for them, too. We all win.

After one of my talks, a young mom, who had heard me before, came up to me. (She came to hear me again, which is always a good sign.) She was excited to tell me that she had started setting her alarm fifteen minutes earlier so she could begin every day with quiet reflections, meditation, and prayer. "I have to do it in my bedroom, before the kids know I'm up."

She explained her routine. "I put my grandmother's rocker in the corner of my bedroom, with my mom's shawl around my shoulders. I light a candle with a lovely scent. Then I read something from the stack of inspirational materials I've been collecting for years. Every day, I rock and read and pray. This fifteen minutes has changed my life. Every day is better. I'm more organized, more productive, more cheerful. You were right about nurturing my mind, body, and spirit…that time is a great investment."

You, too, can combine the physical, mental, and spiritual in simple, creative ways. Take a walk or hike to a peaceful setting, then relax there. Walk or bike to your next appointment, enjoying the sites, nurturing your five senses, clearing your mind.

Sleep in late on a Saturday morning, awaken, and read an inspirational book. Massages, manicures, and herbal baths are lovely ways to nourish the mind, body, and spirit, too.

Take quiet time to examine your life, then politely, with no whining, say, "I want my juice."

Chapter Eight

Wait? It's 108!

Managing Time Wisely

It seemed like hours passed before we arrived at the gates of the airport. Another gun-bearing, mean-looking Vietnamese guard stopped the bus, and our driver motioned for Ross to come forward. Ross began to argue with the guard in Vietnamese. He turned to us and shouted, "President Thieu has canceled our flight. We have to wait for clearance."

Carol and I groaned in unison.

Ross turned back to the guard. "We can't just wait in this bus with all these babies. It's one hundred and eight degrees outside and even hotter in here!" The babies cried even louder since the bus was not in motion.

"These babies are going to lose a lot of fluid in these tears," I shouted over the din, "and the heat will cause diarrhea, which will make them dehydrate for sure!" I scrambled to find the formula. "It's still boiling hot! Now what'll we do?"

Parked in the sun, the van became an oven. We began picking up one baby, then another, in a frenetic effort to comfort as many as possible while Ross continued to appeal to the guard. Perspiration plastered our clothes to us, and sweat dripped from our faces.

As the air inside the bus grew hotter, the little ones grew more frantic. Stroking their damp hair, I blew gently into their faces and waved a diaper as a fan. How sorrowfully ironic that we had cases of formula but nothing to feed the squalling cargo.

Slowly, the bus inched forward through the opening gates.

"They're letting us use the Quonset huts while we wait for this mess to get straightened out," Ross yelled, sounding relieved.

"Maybe we should go back to the center in the meantime, so we can take better care of these babies," Carol called back. "They won't be able to take much more of this."

"No way!" Ross bellowed. "That's just what they want us to do. We are not leaving until the babies are on that plane!"

We carried the infants inside the metal Quonset huts. Their pretty clothes clung to their wet little bodies as they continued to cry. I watched as a little passenger, about five years old, struggled to carry the baby he'd been tending. As the tiny body slid down in his arms, his face grimaced, and his muscles tightened as he clutched the baby closer.

The words to the theme song from the slide show I had presented so many times came to life: "He ain't heavy, he's my brother." I blinked back the tears. How sad that he had to carry one so small. How wonderful that he would.

The old building was filthy inside. Cobwebs and dust hung from the metal walls. We carefully placed the little ones' cut-up cardboard boxes and blankets on the dirty concrete floor. The small windows near the ceiling were so grimy, light could barely shine through.

The sounds of the crying echoed off the sides of the tin walls. When we spotted a water fountain against one wall, we eagerly ran each bottle of formula under the stream to cool it enough for the babies to drink. It was bedlam as everyone shouted and scurried among the crying crowd, trying to feed four or five babies at a time, as we waited…and waited.

I swallowed hard as I looked around at one hundred babies, wet with their own sweat and tears. "These dehydrating babies don't have time for this."

■   ■   ■

Do you sometimes feel you have too many people and too many obligations begging for your attention and your time?

Lack of enough time is said to be the number one stressor for women. How is it possible that with so much technology and so many time-saving devices at our fingertips, we often feel more stressed, more overwhelmed, less in control, and less able to get it all done?

The nation was at war when Franklin Delano Roosevelt said, "Never before have we had so little time in which to do so much."

Sadly, this saying echoes in many of our minds today, as we cope in our "war zones."

Time is the only thing every person in the world has the same amount of. Everybody has just twenty-four hours a day. How we use it is our decision. Yet, how many times do you find yourself saying, "I don't have the time to eat. I don't have time to exercise. I don't have time to pray. I simply don't have time!"

Too frequently, in our flurry to save the children, the whales, and the world, we don't schedule time for ourselves. We don't postpone brushing our teeth until next Tuesday when we have more time. That's how we should approach scheduling downtime for ourselves.

How often, when people ask how you are, do you answer, "Busy"?

Chart Your Time

To examine how you spend your time, draw a big circle on a piece of paper to represent the twenty-four hours of your day. On this pie chart, section off the amount of time you sleep. (Hopefully, this will be about one-third of the circle, i.e., eight hours.) Now pencil off sections according to how you spend the rest of the hours of your day. Working. Driving. Eating. Exercising. Praying. Spending time with family. Watching TV. Email. Internet. Relaxing. Household chores. What else? Take a look at activities on your assignment list from chapter three and be sure they are on your chart. How much time are you devoting to your priorities?

Study this chart carefully, prayerfully. This is the life you have created. Are there things you'd like to change? Make another pie chart, graphing the life you want to lead. Post it where you can see it. Visualize it. Change it. It's your life.

Recently, on a hectic day, I found myself irritated when, in the Wendy's drive-through line, I had to wait four minutes for my hamburger (with lettuce, so I could get my vegetables). I thought, *How did I get so busy in life that waiting four minutes for a meal annoys me?*

Later, I composed an email and attachment to India and was slightly perturbed when I had to wait two full minutes for it to be sent. I'm sure all the Pony Express riders in heaven were less than sympathetic.

We have lots of gadgets and appliances to help our tasks go more quickly, promising that then we'll have time to do the things we love. We have Velcro diapers, faster computers, and microwave ovens that are supposed to make life so much simpler. But, do they? It seems the more time we save, the less we have to spend. The faster and faster and faster we go, the farther and farther and farther it can take us from things that are priorities.

The first car phone and cell phone ads promised that if we used them, we'd have more time to play and be with the people we love. Commercials showed men and women going home, putting their feet up, and hugging their kids and the dog because they got all their work done. But instead, cell phones allow us to work non-stop, in our car, on the bus, in the park, in a restaurant, stealing us from our kids and our dogs.

Log Your Time

Buy or create a daily appointment book and, at the end of the day, record how you spent each of the hours. How did you really spend your time? What do you want to change?

One day, on an hour-long road trip, I happened to follow a car occupied by a woman and four kids. For the entire sixty miles, the driver talked on her cell phone, and I felt sad for her. My car time was sometimes my best time with my kids. (Maybe because I held them captive and they had no choice.) I loved driving them places because they talked then. But they can't talk to us if we're on the phone.

Recently, I read an article titled "Great News for Time-strapped Parents." It reported a kiddie concierge business that would arrange play dates for your child, research the best ballet classes and ball teams, and take them there for you. That didn't sound like great news to me. An adjacent ad suggested that you didn't have to take time to be with your child: You could call him or her on your matching cell phones instead.

Cell phones are, for sure, a mixed blessing. I've chosen only to have mine on when I'm on the road, so my clients and family can reach me. No one else has my number. I figure, it's my device, I can control when and if I utilize it, and I vow, I will never have one attached to my head! I won't text message. I check my email only once a day when I'm on the road. I refuse to use a

Blackberry or a Palm Pilot. Using a nut pick to type in a schedule that dictates my life is not right for me.

What's right for you?

Often, a lot of our time is spent collecting stuff. We work long and hard so we can collect more stuff. We build big houses so we can fill them up, then we build three- and four-car garages so we can fill them up, and then we rent storage units so we can fill them up. Think of the number of packages of stuff you carry into your house in a week. How many sacks do you carry out? It is said we can remove one grocery sack full of stuff we don't need any more from our homes every week, not counting garbage. If you haven't done that, it means you have fifty-two extra bags of stuff in your house this year. That explains my basement and my closets.

Some people go on vacation to get away from their stuff. Think how you feel in a motel room, when all you have are the bare essentials. Do you experience a sense of relief when your life feels streamlined and uncluttered? Do you really need to spend more time collecting more material goods? When is enough, enough?

Psychologists Ed Diener and Martin E.P. Seligman analyzed more than 150 studies on wealth and happiness and found that economic indicators have glaring shortcomings when it comes to determining how happy people are. They report that, in many countries, "although economic output has risen steeply over the past decades, there has been no rise in life satisfaction...and there has been a substantial increase in depression and distrust.... Economic success falls short as a measure of well-being, in part because materialism can negatively influence well-being, and also because it is possible to be happy without living a life of luxury."

There's a story of how children in the jungles catch monkeys. From a tree branch, they hang a gourd with a small hole cut in it, just the size of a monkey's flat hand. Then, inside it, they put "stuff" monkeys love. The monkeys come, reach in, and grab the delectable stuff in their fists. But they can't get their hands out! Will they let go to save their lives? Never! And they're captured. Are you captured by not letting go of your stuff?

Feng shui, the ancient Chinese system for creating harmony in our environment, warns against the surplus of material goods. Its first rule is, no clutter. Most faith traditions extol simplicity as a means to spiritual enlightenment. In Roman Catholicism, austerity, exemplified by monks and nuns, was held for centuries as a model. Buddhism stresses the relationship between external simplicity and internal insight.

Lifestyle experts and religious leaders describe a growing appreciation by many Americans that an overabundance of goods can be a drag on spiritual development. Increasingly, decluttering and downsizing are being viewed in a spiritual context, as ways to remove distractions from inner growth. People are realizing that the more they have, the more they have to take responsibility for, leaving less time for the breathing space of God.

These lessons are important to teach our children, too. Remember, we are always role modeling, and we need to show them that we…and they…cannot have it all, so we'd better teach them now.

Life is about choices. They need to choose between gym and

> *Overall* **free time** *for children has declined twelve hours per week over the last ten eyars, according to a study from the Survey Research Center at the University of Michigan. Unstructured outdoor activities, such as walking, hiking, or camping, fell by 50 percent.*

soccer and Girl Scouts and 4-H and dance and music lessons and baseball. We've created a "hurried-child" trend in this country by hyper-scheduling our kids. Busyness has become a status symbol. Downtime is seen as anti-American.

Like us, children need space for silence and contemplation for their mental health.

Though teens typically rebuff parental overtures, they want parents to keep trying. In a national YMCA poll of American teens, 21 percent rated "not having enough time together with parents" as their top concern. This tied with educational worries as their chief concern.

Although the average child spends six to eight hours a day on "screen time," once he or she starts school, the average parent and child interact just twelve minutes a day, six of which are negative.

Researchers at John J. Heldrich Center for Workforce Development at Rutgers University surveyed one thousand workers around the country, and 95 percent said they are concerned about spending more time with their families.

So what is stopping them?

When the typical person is asked whether they feel more time-poor or money-poor, the answer is almost always time-poor.

Whereas 28 percent of dual-earner parents said they play or exercise with their children every day, only a miniscule 6 percent of kids agreed that was the case, says Ellen Galinsky of the Families and Work Institute.

The Families and Work Institute says 33 percent of women and 28 percent of men would prefer to work part-time if they could afford it.

They must have figured out that even if you win the rat race, you're still a rat.

If you chase money, it may catch you—if it catches you, you'll forever be its slave.

We have a lot more control of our time than we exercise. It took me too long to realize how I was putting myself under undue pressure. I used to leave a message on my business answering machine saying I would be back by a specific hour to return my calls. Then I found myself rushing through snarled traffic or shoving a grocery cart at break-neck speed so I could meet my own self-imposed deadlines! Finally, I learned to say I would be back "mid-afternoon." This tiny change reduced my stress immensely.

My time is precious, and I hate to waste it. Some people are penny-pinchers; I'm a minute-pincher. Are you like me? If it takes twenty minutes to get to an appointment, do you leave exactly twenty minutes before you're to be there? It took years of New Year's resolutions to discipline myself to leave just five minutes earlier so I'm under less pressure en route. Try it. If you arrive a few minutes early, read from your motivational or inspirational books, kept in the car for this sacred time.

A recent article reported about the hundreds of hours Americans are forced to waste each year, in lines and in traffic. I admonished myself, wondering, why does this time have to be time wasted? We can use it to listen to positive or inspirational

Tips to Slow Down

1) Leave holes in your daily calendar instead of filling every minute. Easing the pressure on your time allows you to slow down.

2) Monitor your pace. Don't move quickly out of habit.

3) Take a deep breath and consciously slow down.

4) Eat all meals sitting down at a table. Never stand to eat.

5) Make time for at least one hobby that allows you to slow down.

6) Turn off all technology and noise for a specified time each day. Sit quietly.

CDs, to practice positive visualization, to hum a spiritual song, or sing the soundtrack from *Camelot*.

Remember when Sundays and Sabbaths were days of rest? Stores were closed. Life slowed down. No matter how many crops needed to be planted or harvested, my daddy didn't work. And neither did mom, after she prepared the Sunday dinner. Sunday was a day to rest, to read under the elm tree, to visit friends. Won't it be wonderful to reclaim that? To have one day when we are not "busy."

These stinging words from Max Lucado reminded me of the danger of being too busy: "Busyness rapes relationships. It substitutes shallow frenzy for deep friendships. It promises satisfying dreams but delivers hollow nightmares. It feeds the ego but fractures a family. It cultivates a program, but plows under priorities."

We can choose to slow down. I had a burlap wall hanging in the sixties (boy, now I'm really dating myself), and the felt letters read, "Take time to smell the flowers."

Georgia O'Keeffe, one of the greatest painters of flowers, said, "Nobody ever really sees a flower, it is so small, they haven't time. And to really see it takes time. Like having a friend takes time."

Make a vow from this day forward that you are not going to spend your time, you are going to invest it, according to your priorities and your choices. You'll nurture your flowers, your friends, your families, and yourself.

Chapter Nine

I'm Not Leaving without My Son!

Living Our Priorities

The muggy air inside the Quanset hut threatened to smother our efforts. Carol ran the bottles of formula under water at the drinking fountain, handed them to me one at a time, and I fed babies as fast as I could.

Finally, Ross returned with the latest word from airport officials. "President Thieu will let only this one plane load of orphans leave."

Quickly, I began to gather babies and head for the bus. Ross stopped me. "You didn't hear me, LeAnn. I said one plane. To be sure you see Mark and your girls again, you have got to get on this one."

"What about the rest of the babies?" I refused to hear his message. "What about Mitch?"

Ross put his hands on my shoulders and stared into my eyes. "I'm staying, LeAnn, and I promise I'll try to get him and bring him to you in the States. But now you have got…to…go…home."

I stepped into his arms, buried my head in his chest, and bawled like the babies.

My frantic mind tried to think of what to do. Then I remembered my priorities: my family.

"I'm not leaving without my son!"

"Do you know what you're saying?"

I threw my arms in the air. "I can't go home without him!"

"Go, then," Ross said. "I'll try to hold the plane until you get back."

I knew he would be powerless to do so, but he explained the plan to the bus driver as I climbed its stairs two at a time.

The same bus that crept so slowly en route to the airport now sped rapidly, almost recklessly back toward the center with me as its only passenger. The crowded streets, the hundreds of weaving bicycles, the lane-less convoy of cars angered me as the bus honked and jerked through the snarled traffic.

Why couldn't they hurry?

Why couldn't they clear a path?

Didn't they know that this was literally a matter of life and death?

Already I couldn't imagine my life without Mitchell.

Finally, the driver stopped on the main street, opened the door, smiled, and pointed down the narrow road ahead. I jumped off the bus and raced down the dirt street toward the center.

Breathless, I ran and prayed out loud. "Please, God, please let me get there in time to get Mitch and get back."

The strap of my sandal broke. My shoe flopped wildly against my ankle. I grabbed it without breaking stride, clenched it in my fist, and ran in one bare foot, with all my might.

"Please, Lord," I wheezed. "My family is my priority. Now Mitch is family. Please let them hold the plane!"

My side ached fiercely as I pushed harder. The center was in sight. Numbness and burning fired through my legs. Panting and puffing, I ran through the courtyard gates, up the steps, and into the office. Cherie looked up, startled.

"I've got to get Mitch! I've got to get back!'

Cherie interrupted. "I know, I know," she said, easing me into a chair. "I just got off the phone with the government and the airport. They're holding the plane."

I beamed a smile while gasping for breath.

She waited for me to catch my wind before she continued. Officials had notified her that the flight would wait for additional babies, and a second flight was approved to leave, too.

Still panting, I hurried into the next room. Across the nursery I saw Mitch, waiting in a white shirt and red checkered playsuit. I'd only been his mom for three days, but he raised his arms to me as if to say, "I never doubted you for a minute, Mom."

■ ■ ■

What are the priorities in your life?

Truly living our priorities can be a real challenge. Periodically, we need to re-evaluate.

Make a list of what is most important to you. Include all areas of life—family—faith—friends—fitness—finances—community. Each of these is important and deserving of your attention.

Which is the *number one* priority?

Are you living it?

I might challenge you a bit when I suggest that priorities are not what we state them to be but how we're actually spending our time. We can't give lip service to one thing and say it's our priority if we are spending our time doing something else. Obviously, what we're spending our time doing is what we have established as our priority, is it not?

I always thought I was living my priorities when one day a friend asked me what mine was. Without missing a beat, I said, "Mark and my kids."

My friend asked, "Do you spend much time with your children?"

I answered confidently, "Yes, I do. That's why Mark and I agreed I'd work part-time."

"Do you spend much time listening to them?"

"You'd better believe it!" I smirked. "From six o'clock in the morning to eight o'clock at night, they're talking, I'm listening."

"How much time," he asked, "do you spend looking them in the eyes and listening?"

Oops! I considered how often, while listening, I was also talking on the phone or peeling potatoes or sorting papers. I began to wonder, *Do my little kids know they are the number one priority in my life, or do they sometimes feel like they're competing with peeled potatoes and papers?*

So, starting then, every day, I made a point to stop what I was doing, look them in the eye, and listen, if only for a few minutes at a time. I could tell immediately how much they loved it.

Then I had a revelation. I wonder if this could apply to my spouse? I realized I wasn't looking Mark in the face and listening either! It was about this same time I recalled what a wise old nurse had taught me after I had delivered Christie. Before I left the hospital, she reminded me to pay attention to my husband, too. She said, "Every day when he comes home, you need to show him that he is still number one in your life, even though you've had a baby. So when he walks through that door, have nothing in your arms, go to him, put your arms around him, and tell him that you love him."

Nice idea, I thought, but not very realistic when you have kids. Still, I believed it was important. I knew that one day, after one hundred years or so of child rearing, it would be just the two of us again, and I had to keep our love alive in the meantime. So I began. The first day he came home and I wrapped my arms around him, he said. "Oh, oh, what's the matter?"

I said, "Nothing. I just love you."

"I love you, too. Did the water heater leak again?"

After a few days of this, he figured out there was no catch, it was just my loving routine. And soon it became his, too.

Mark was way ahead of me on making our marriage a priority. When the kids were little, he insisted we have date night once a week. It turned out it had to be on Thursdays because that's when the high-school babysitter was free. But the night of the week or the place of the date didn't matter. During one lean period, we only could afford a cone at Dairy Queen, but the conversation and love were delicious.

Living our priorities can mean gestures as simple as that. Kids are often our best teachers.

A friend of mine was hurriedly packing to catch a plane for a business trip when his four-year-old son came into the room and asked, "Daddy, can I tell you something?" He said, "Sure, buddy, if you can talk fast." His little boy said, "That's okay, Daddy. I'll wait 'til you can listen slow."

If partners and kids aren't your chosen priorities at this time in your life, remember, these principles still apply. If your priority is your self-care, your extended family, or your community work, are your devoting your time and attention there?

To live your priorities, it helps to be in the moment. Whether it's while you're pushing a child in a swing, listening to a friend, or making love, how often is your mind on the next business deal, the dinner menu, or overdrawn bank account? Too often we miss the joy of simple things because our minds are miles away.

Were you shocked to learn that the average parent and child in this country spend twelve minutes a day one-on-one, six of which are negative? How does that happen? Too often, people invest their time and energy on things that are going well for them, and they divest it, take it away, from things that aren't going so well. So, if things aren't going easily at home or with the kids, they invest their time and energy at work, where they see they can make improvements. In doing this, they are frequently taking themselves away from the very thing they claimed to be their priority. I don't believe this happens on purpose but so gradually they hardly recognize it.

Like the story you may have heard about a frog: If you place a frog in a vat of boiling water (don't call the ASPCA—we wouldn't really do this!), it immediately jumps out to save its life. But if you put a frog in a vat of cold water and very slowly turn up the heat, it gets hotter and hotter and hotter, and the frog dies there because the change was so gradual it didn't sense the danger.

Are there negative changes happening to your commitment to priorities? If so, turn down the heat.

It's important to remember we are always juggling balls of responsibility in our lives. It's crucial to determine which of these are rubber and which are glass. The rubber ones...which are often all our "stuff," our committees, even our jobs...if they are dropped, they can bounce back or be replaced. The glass ones...which are usually our health and those we love...if they are broken, they are irretrievably broken.

Don't drop them.

How we spend our time is truly an indicator of how we live our priorities, isn't it? The faster and faster we go, the farther and farther it can take us from our priorities, if we aren't careful.

A simple (not easy, but simple) gesture for living priorities is to resurrect the family supper. (Whether you have children or not, you are still a family.)

I was a stickler about this when the kids were home, and I must admit the importance was not as clear to them at the time as it was to me. It was often a pain in the tush to rearrange dinner around ballet, baseball, Boy Scouts, and horse poop. But we had supper together, even if it was at 7:30. They didn't grumble about it often, because the expectation had been set long before, and they knew it was non-negotiable.

Kids who have 5–7 family dinners per week are:
- *At 70 percent lower risk for substance abuse;*
- *Half as likely to try cigarettes or marijuana;*
- *One-third less likely to try alcohol;*
- *Half as likely to get drunk monthly.*

Kids who frequently eat dinner with their families are also likelier to have better grades and confide in their parents, reports Columbia University's National Center on Addiction and Substance Abuse.

Family meals say to our children, "Being with you is important to me. Nothing else matters more." Our children are craving to hear that. Remember the statistic about the 429 kids who wanted more time with their parents, doing simple things together? Mealtime is a perfect time for that. Obeying the rule of only positive talk at the table allows for wonderful conversations and connectedness.

Dear Abby (there she is again) said, "If you want great kids, spend twice as much time with them and half as much on them."

I'm glad the 70s theory that it's not the quantity of time you spend with your child but the quality has been disproved. I never bought it anyway. That doesn't make sense in other areas of our lives, so why should it be relevant to our children? Imagine that you have been looking forward to having the Mile High Double Chocolate Brownie Ice Cream Chocolate Chip Dessert with Fudge Sauce all day. But when you get to the gourmet ice cream shop, the waiter brings you a one-inch chocolate piece in a pretty foil wrapper. When you complain, she says, "Ma'am, I recognize this portion is small, but this is the finest chocolate money can buy; you'll find none better in the world. I hope you understand, it's not the quantity but the quality that counts." You'd never accept that explanation, and neither should our children. They deserve both.

Until we make the proper raising of our children the number one priority of our nation, we will continue to have social woes.

People without children have an important, irreplaceable role in the raising or our children, too. Aunts, uncles, Big Brothers, and Big Sisters can often impact a child's life in a way that parents cannot.

> It costs *four times* as much to send a kid to the state pen as it does to send him to Penn State.

There is an African tribal greeting, used between neighboring tribes, "*Abantwani Joni.*" It means, "How are the children?" Africans have known for some time what Americans are learning: the health of the nation, community, and family depends on the health of children.

We should all be alarmed to read studies showing that the majority of juvenile crimes and pregnancies are not conceived in the dark of the night, but from 3:00 to 6:00 in the afternoon. With 70 percent of mothers of school-age children working, there are at least five million children whose parents admit their kids are in "self-care."

Mother Teresa feared, "Children have no time for parents. Parents have no time for each other. In the home begins the disruption of world peace."

Lest I be misunderstood, I am not advocating that mothers not work outside the home. I've watched my generation struggle with this dilemma. In the 70s we donned our business pant suits

A survey by The National Commission of Working Women showed that although 93 percent of teenagers say they expect to work as adults, 50 percent of girls and 60 percent of boys said one parent would stay home to raise the kids

and even neck ties to claim our places in the corporate world. If we didn't "work" in the 80s, we were made to feel that we had abandoned "the Cause." In the 90s corporate women who never had kids were often frustrated, and Supermoms verged on nervous breakdowns. Finally, in this new millennium, women care less about what others think and are doing what's right for them and their families. The old terms of "ambitious" and "driven" are no longer compliments, and the word "homemaker" can be stated with pride, for what better job could there be than to make a home.

Every woman—and every family—needs to evaluate their employment plans individually. I tried working full-time temporarily, for only a month or so. I felt like I was a lousy mother, lover, wife, nurse, and me. I tried staying home for two years, raising babies. When I began to cut Mark's meat at the table while talking baby talk, I knew it was time to find a balance. For me, it was always part-time work. My sister tried this same approach and learned that she was her best working full-time. Every family needs to figure that out and be open to flexibility to make it happen and to change it again if needed.

I watched families in my childbirth classes sell their five bedroom tri-levels to buy two bedroom duplexes so dad could stay home to care for the baby. Conversely, more often I saw early pregnant couples buy a new home with more bedrooms plus an SUV for the car seat. Then in postpartum class I watched mom weep because she "had" to go back to work. It seems unjust that often men and women are caught in the double bind of starting a family at the very same time they're expected to climb the career ladder.

The effect of income on life satisfaction seems transient, researchers say. Once people get past the poverty level, money does not play a role in day-to-day happiness, says Alan Krueger, a professor of economics and public affairs at Princeton University.

Perhaps success isn't the person who has the most things but the one who needs less. As I was wrestling with this in my life, I read a quotation that drilled home the priority message: Success is measured by how your child describes you to a friend.

Success—"To laugh often and love much; to win the respect of intelligent persons and the affection of children; to earn the approbation of honest citizens and endure the betrayal of false friends; to appreciate beauty; to find the best in others; to give of one's self; to leave the world a bit better, whether by a healthy child, a garden patch or a redeemed social condition; to have played and laughed with enthusiasm and sung with exultation; to know even one life has breathed easier because you have lived—this is to have succeeded."—Ralph Waldo Emerson

While we were applying for adoption for Mitch, we shopped for a bigger house. I found the perfect one, only a few thousand dollars over our budgeted amount. I reasoned that I could work three days a week, instead of my current two, and pick up extra shifts so we could afford it. Our realtor gave us sage advice when he posed this question: "Will you own your house, or will it own you?"

We knew the house would own us. We made one of those "right decisions" and, sure enough, God took care of the rest. We found an even more perfect house within our budget.

Do you have "stuff" that owns you?

Some people lose their health to make more money, then lose their money to restore their health. If you chase money, it may catch you. And if it catches you, you will be its slave forever.

We've all heard adages such as, "Are you making a living or making a life?" And, "Few people on their death beds say they wish they'd have spent more time at the office." The one that struck me most was, "Tombstones don't say, *She Was #1 in the Region,* they say, *Beloved Mother, Wife, and Friend.*"

Audrey Hepburn was the spokesperson for UNICEF when she said, "Take care of the small circle around you. When you have succeeded with them, then step out, one small step at a time."

This principle applies to all the priorities on your list, whatever they may be: your spouse, yourself, your faith, your service.

Too often we are so busy striving, we don't allow ourselves to "arrive." Our happiness, we believe, is dependent on external things: "I'll be happy when I have more stuff, the kids are happy, I have a better job...." True happiness does not come from outer but inner abundance.

At various phases of our lives, we must step back and reexamine our priorities and how we are living them. I was blessed to work only part-time while the kids were at home. Our "price" for that was living in a small, though wonderful, three-bedroom ranch home and driving used cars. A simple price we happily paid. When Mitch flew the coop and our nest was empty, that's when my speaking and writing hobby catapulted into a full-time busy career. Suddenly, this stay-at-home-mom was jet-setting across the nation, gone eighty nights a year, which was expected to double fast. The bookings and the books came rolling in, and it was time to decide: I could leave my home office, rent space and hire several full-time staff and make a ton more money, or I could keep my office at home next to Mark's, my half-time virtual assistant, my sanity, and happy marriage. I examined my priorities, my life assignments and chose the latter.

Just because we can, doesn't mean we should.

Now, my #1 priority is keeping my #1 priority my #1 priority. What's yours?

Chapter Ten

I Can't Work Fast Enough!

Managing Stress

We carried the babies into a mammoth C-5 cargo jet, where all but a few seats had been removed. Down the center, twenty cardboard boxes, each approximately two feet square, sat side by side. Two to three babies lay in each box. A long strap stretched from one end of the plane, over the boxes, and attached to the other end. A whole new definition of seatbelt safety. Several large metal trashcans stood at each end with food, formula, and supplies for the trip. The few toddlers and older children sat belted in on the long side benches…bewildered orphans strapped inside a flying boxcar.

The captain instructed the nine adults to buckle up for take-off. I sat with Mitchell on my lap in one of the few seats near the cabin. The sound of the engine's roar was nearly deafening. A panic came over me. My heart raced, and my breath stuck in my chest. Although no words were spoken, each escort must have known what the other was thinking. The last planeload of orphans leaving Saigon blew up shortly after takeoff. It was still unclear whether it had been shot down or sabotaged.

Would ours explode too?

My shaking arms gripped Mitchell close to me. He hugged me back as if to comfort me. The image of the black fiery cloud refueled the terror I had felt when the plane had crashed.

I began to pray as the plane taxied down the runway. I knew if we lived through the next five minutes, Mitch and I would make it home to Iowa. To Mark. To my girls. The motion of the plane lulled the infants to near silence. The adults sat statue-like. Only the engine's vengeful roar broke the haunting, threatening stillness.

I felt the plane lift off the ground.

My heart thumped faster. I prayed faster.

Finally, the captain spoke. "We are out of range of the Vietcong. We are safe. We are going home!"

Shouts of gladness and relief filled the plane. I continued to pray, almost laughing, this time in thanksgiving. The weight of fear lifted from my chest and shoulders. I stood Mitchell on my lap to face me. "We're going home, son."

Immediately, we adults unfastened our seatbelts and hastened to tend to the babies. Several helpers were Air Force personnel. Others were Americans taking advantage of the opportunity to get out of the country fast.

One burly man with huge hands and salt-and-pepper hair leaned over a box and began changing a diaper. He admitted this was his first, which was obvious, and we laughed with him as he did it clumsily.

Someone whispered, "His wife was killed in the crash a few days ago." No wonder his eyes looked so anxious.

By now all one hundred babies were crying simultaneously. The formula was a perfect temperature, just as the worker had planned, and we propped countless bottles to rehydrate the little ones. We quickly learned to feed all three babies in a box at the same time by placing them on their sides and propping their bottles on the shoulders of their box-mates. Some sucked the formula down in only minutes while others needed more help. I cradled a baby girl in my folded legs and coaxed her to drink while using my other hand to feed another baby. The nipple fell from the mouth of the one in my lap. Clearly, she was too weak to suckle. Using both hands, I milked formula from the nipple to her mouth. While other babies protested, I continued until an ounce was taken.

Though it was difficult work, a sense of merriment danced between us volunteers…we were taking children to freedom, to families.

As the bottles emptied, we draped diapers over our shoulders and burped two at a time.

Soon, the predicted diarrhea diapers became a reality, and we changed one after the other. The handsome burly man wrinkled his face as he dangled a dirty mess between his thumb and index finger and took it to the assigned trash can.

With one in my arms and two in my lap, I held and fed three infants at a time. Then I noticed the baby girl with a cleft palate, crying so hard she was hoarse. I picked up the wee one, and she rested limply in my lap. It didn't take a pediatric nurse to diagnose exhaustion and dehydration. Drop by drop, I squeezed formula from the bottle through her deformed lip. The engine roared, the babies wailed, the walls vibrated, my heart ached, and my stress escalated as I listened to ninety-nine babies protest while I gave undivided attention to one.

■ ■ ■

Do you sometimes feel that you have too many people and too many obligations begging for your attention and your time?

Lack of enough time is said to be the number one stressor for women. How is it possible that with so much technology and so many time-saving devices at our fingertips, we often feel more stressed, more overwhelmed, less in control, and less able to get it all done? My grandma used to say, "The hurrier I go, the behinder I get." Although you will rarely do laundry for a family of ten in a ringer-washing machine and hang it on the clothesline, and you may never have to feed one hundred squalling babies at a time, I'm guessing you can relate to how grandma and I felt under stress.

Lack of enough time is a major stressor. Stress causes anxiety, fear, frustration, and loss of self-control, all of which diminish our productivity and self-worth.

When you're running late and the carpool is honking and the phone is ringing and the lunches aren't packed and your lipstick isn't on yet and the phone is ringing and your child just now remembers a note to be signed for today's field trip and the phone is ringing and your teenager talks back to you…you snap, say something you regret, and everyone's self-worth is damaged.

The impact that stress has on your life is not determined by your exposure to stress but by your response to it.

Halted traffic, rude tellers, or incompetent coworkers do not cause your heart to pound or your blood pressure to rise; your response does.

My mama was right: "You can't always control the situation; you can only control your reaction to it." Life is inherently stressful. Some of the stress we can identify and eliminate.

What we do with the rest is our decision.

Big stressors kick us into the "fight-or-flight mode" we discussed earlier. Our bodies are designed to produce adrenalin to get us through the crisis and then to calm down. That in itself is not hard on us. It's fighting the tiger and never settling down that causes problems. Research shows damage is not done by ordinary stress but by chronic and persistent stress with no recovery periods. The happiest, healthiest, most productive people are those who oscillate back and forth between stress and recovery. They work hard and play hard, go and then let go, become active and then rest.

It's important to remember that not all stress is bad. There is a good kind called eustress. I'd heard of euphoria, but I hadn't heard of eustress. It's a positive kind of stress that all life forms have, the kind that keeps life changing and productive when everything around it is changing. So we need some stress, But enough already!

The US Surgeon General reported that 80 percent of non-traumatic deaths in this country are stress-related.

Cleveland Clinic says 75 percent to 90 percent of all doctors' office visits are for stress-related ailments.

The Occupational Safety and Health Administration (OSHA) declared stress a hazard of the workplace, costing American industry more than $300 billion a year.

1,500 separate documented physical changes occur in the human body in response to stress, resulting in everything from suppression of the immune system to depression and eating disorders. In stress, a hormone called cortisol is released, which causes, among other things, poor judgment and forgetfulness. Chronically high levels of stress-related hormones can shrink a part of the brain, impairing memory in older people. Too much stress results in ulcers, high blood pressure, headaches, and heart irregularities.

Do you have too much stress? How would I know? you ask. I've been this way so long.

Well, there are symptoms of too much stress. Which apply to you?

Symptoms of Stress

PHYSICAL	MENTAL	SPIRITUAL
Appetite changes	Forgetfulness	Emptiness
Headaches	Poor concentration	Loss of meaning
Fatigue	Dull senses	Doubt
Poor sleeping	Lethargy	Martyrdom
Frequent illnesses	Boredom	Loss of direction
Digestive problems	Low productivity	Cynicism
Pounding heart	Negative attitude	Apathy
Teeth grinding	Anxiety	Abandonment
Rash	The "blues"	Worry
Restlessness	Mood swings	Isolation
Foot-tapping	Anger	Distrust
Finger drumming	Bad dreams	"No one cares"
Smoking	Irritability	
Increased alcohol intake	Crying spells	
	Nervous laughter	
	Loss of loving feeling	

Whether you identified two or twenty of these symptoms, you'll benefit from:

Ways to Reduce Stress

■ *First, identify the triggers. Make a list of situations that cause you stress. Although you can't jump to the head of the line at the grocery store or wish the traffic jam away or convince your husband to clean up his kitchen mess, you can control how you react to these things.*

■ *Review the list you wrote in chapter three, of activities that consume your time. Which of those can be eliminated or delegated?*

■ *Reduce the noise around you. Turn down or shut off televisions, radios, or rowdy kids.*

■ *Avoid rushing. Leave sooner. Get up earlier.*

■ *Plan ahead. Don't let the gas tank get below one-fourth of a tank. Keep staples stocked in the kitchen. Don't wait until you use your last bus token or postage stamp to buy more, etc.*

■ *Review your pie chart of how you spend your time in a day. What can you change?*

■ *Stay healthy. Eat, sleep, exercise so you are strong and can manage better.*

■ *Stay positive. Keep away from grumpy negative people. Choose positive ones.*

■ *Pray and meditate every day.*

■ *Repair or replace things that don't work properly (family members not included).*

■ *Don't rely on your memory. Write things down.*

■ *Break big tasks into bite-sized manageable portions.*

■ *Unclutter and organize, so you can easily find things.*

■ *Simplify, simplify, simplify.*

■ *Quit trying to "fix" other people.*

■ *Lower your standards and expectations. Some things aren't worth doing perfectly. Shoot for sevens—we can't always score a ten.*

Okay, now you've reduced it as much as you can. Here are ways to cope with the remaining stress:

Ways to Cope with Stress

■ *Smile, even if you don't feel like it, and hold it for thirty seconds. Smiling releases endorphins, giving you calm and control.*

■ *Do your relaxation breathing and visualization exercises.*

■ *Visualize yourself responding to the stressor in a calm, empowered manner.*

■ *Take time out. Pop in a CD of relaxation, humor, or easy listening music.*

■ *Exercise. At work, find a stairwell. Or put a file under your arm and walk quickly on your "urgent assignment."*

■ *Get outdoors. Walk. Fresh air and nature's breezes help blow stress away.*

■ *Pray. My mom sent me a greeting card that read, "God helps us in timesof stress, to live at our magnificent best."*

■ *Eat right. Add extra protein for more energy.*

■ *Sleep. Too often we deprive ourselves of sleep during stressful times, yet it is a critical recovery tool.*

■ *Sing. When dealing with stress-related problems, African shaman ask, "When did you stop singing?"*

■ *Share your feelings with others or in a journal.*

■ *Believe in your ability to cope. Embrace your strengths. Create an action plan to deal with stressors.*

Imagine if your energy was not being taken up with stress, what you would be capable of! There's no reason to be stretched to the breaking point in your everyday life. Regain control of how you respond to stress. No more snapping.

Reclaim your calm.

Chapter Eleven

I Only Intended to Buy a Dozen Cupcakes

Making a Difference

After nearly five hours of feeding, burping, and changing, the pilot announced we would stop in the Philippines to refuel. That didn't sound unrealistic to our crew, but the news that we would be detained for each baby to have a medical checkup caused complaining.

"Why don't they just let us get to Oakland as soon as possible, where the babies can get care?" I muttered to a co-worker.

I felt a little selfish when she answered, "Some babies could be in critical condition if they had to wait until then."

My eagerness to get home had overshadowed my logic.

The plane made a smooth landing on the runway of Clark Air Force Base. Babies gently bumped against each other as the plane came to a halt. Looking out the window, I was surprised to see dozens of women on the landing strip, obviously there to help with our mission. One by one they entered the back door of the plane and exited the front, each carrying a baby.

"We're US military wives," a pretty blonde explained as she took an infant from Ross. "We're thrilled to be a part of this," she said, nodding toward the fussing cargo.

Another woman approached me and reached to take Mitchell from my arms.

"Oh, no, you don't," I protested with a laugh.

She smiled politely. "We're under strict instructions to take every baby from the plane. No exceptions, I'm afraid."

I clutched him closer to me. "No. I'm his mom."

She persisted. "Each child must be checked in, according to the government airlift plan."

She reached for him again, and I gently pushed her hand away. "You don't understand what I've been through to get him." My voice broke. "I almost lost him once. Never again."

Carol and Ross came to convince me to let him go. "We escorts are to be taken to a nice motel, where we can clean up and rest. Then you'll be with him again," Carol assured me.

"I don't want to go to a nice motel. I want to be with my son," I pouted, then reluctantly handed Mitchell to the stranger.

I kissed him in her arms. "Mommy will be there soon, honey."

He didn't seem to oppose the separation, but my arms and heart felt empty without him.

Deep down I knew it was probably best. I felt weak, and my cramping was increasing again.

We deplaned and walked across the hot pavement. The air felt fresher and less humid, though as hot as in Saigon. We were ushered into a dimly lit building off the tarmac, where women in American Red Cross uniforms greeted us. Because telephone communication was nearly impossible in Vietnam, their primary purpose was to call our families to let them know of our safe arrival.

One lady in a uniform smiled and said, "I understand this planeload of one hundred babies is just a start—there are more planes and more children coming."

"We have another two hundred babies that should be here tomorrow," Ross said hopefully.

A gray-haired worker added, "The news reported that London sent a Boeing 707 to Saigon for 150 orphans."

"I heard Australia flew out over two hundred," the lady in the red vest offered.

"We can vouch for that!" Carol attested. "We were there and put some of our babies on that plane."

"Another sixty-three went to Canada, and fifty more to West Germany," another chimed in.

"Wow," I breathed, barely comprehending the magnitude of this adventure.

The lady in the red vest put her arm around my shoulder. "Volunteering to save hundreds of babies was extraordinary."

I smiled meekly. "I volunteered for six."

She seemed startled. "It wasn't your intention from the start to help rescue hundreds?"

I thought of the bake sale booth in the mall several years ago. I shook my head and chuckled.

"All I originally intended to do was buy a dozen cupcakes."

▪   ▪   ▪

Like me, do you ever start out to do something small and then find it gets really big and you have no idea how you ever got so involved?

As we strive to make a difference in this world, we need to make healthy, conscious decisions about how involved to be, or our lives get way out of balance.

We can choose to respond to the needy in three ways.

No Involvement

You may know some people with this approach or lack thereof. I like to think it is not from an absence of caring but an absence of knowledge. It's a lot easier not to do something about a problem if you don't know about it. It's a lot easier not to do something if you don't know that every year over five million kids die in our world from poor nutrition. That's the population of Scotland.

> *2.5 million children in the world die every year for lack of diarrhea medicine.*

Lest we think that the USA escapes these problems, thirty million people in our country do not have enough to eat or must scrounge for food.

Occasionally, I have heard those who choose not to be involved say, "They should pull themselves up by their bootstraps," forgetting that some have no boots.

Others say, "They should take care of their own." I've never understood how manmade geographical boundaries should determine which children in the world survive.

> *The two hundred wealthiest people in the world have more money than the two billion poorest.*

I suspect the main reason most choose not to be involved is because the problems seem too overwhelming; their part would be insignificant. An old Chinese proverb says, "If you want to leave footprints in the sand, you can't sit on your butt—who wants to leave butt prints in the sand?"

Idealism is one of my quirks, I admit, but I've often thought that if every person on Earth did two hours of volunteer work per week, soon there would be no causes left in the world. I believe that no effort is too small. Every action matters. An ancient

Creole Haitian proverb proves that, stating, "Even one cockroach's urine helps make the river rise."

I prefer different imagery that makes the same point. There was a sign above a burn unit in Vietnam where an American plastic surgeon set up a clinic to help those kids burned and disfigured by the war. Engraved above the doorway were the words: "It's better to light a single candle than to curse the darkness."

But, it doesn't have to be a Roman candle!

That's the second way we serve.

Over Involvement

Reluctantly, I admit that was probably what I was bordering on when I left for Vietnam: "over involvement." Our well-meaning, zealous attempts to help the less fortunate sometimes detract us from our priorities (see chapter nine). Sometimes, it seems easier to right the wrongs of the world than to make things right at home. Over involvement fractures our families, hampers our health, and maligns our minds.

Doing too much good can go bad, depleting us physically, mentally, and spiritually.

So there must be another way, a third way, to make a difference, and that is, of course, a balanced way.

Balanced Involvement

There is, indeed, a time for every purpose under heaven. After the airlift, I did not take on any big causes until our kids were in high school (then, I nearly got in over my head again!). I'd learned a lesson—in order to be the mom and wife I wanted to be, I had to limit my involvement. But I also learned there are marvelous ways of doing that while still making a difference in the world. I did little things like the annual cancer drives in our neighborhood and dropping coins in every single red kettle at Christmas time.

Being good stewards of our earth and our possessions is a simple way to make a difference. Recycling and giving away "stuff" we aren't using is an easy way to care. Why would we ever throw away something someone else could use?

Since we are always role modeling, we can teach our children, in subtle ways, these principles and that we *are* called to be our brothers' keepers. Sparing children from this is doing a disservice, because it robs them of opportunities to identify their gifts and share them.

> *"Many have discovered helping others to be the most enduring therapy, for it's the burden you help another to bear that makes your own seem light."*
>
> *—Albert Schweitzer*

We sponsored a child in Africa, and our kids pledged a portion of their meager allowances to send to Musa. His letters telling of their bountiful harvest—nearly seven bags of grain—impacted us all.

A dear friend taught her children to tithe ten cents from every dollar they earned and put it in a special jar. She contributed the same portion from her writing income, and her husband from his business. Twice a year, the kids explored causes and selected a favorite. Together they wrote the check, walked to the mailbox, and sent their caring.

Tithing is a balanced way to make a difference, but it was one of my hardest lessons to learn. For years I believed our family had only enough to meet our own needs, and I looked forward to the day when we would earn more so we could tithe regularly. Yet every time I looked into the face of a starving poster child, I had a hard time explaining to him that I was sorry he was so hungry, but the Little League dues, ballet tutus, and karate lessons consumed every available dollar. To ease my conscience, we added up all the money we donated to Musa, Save the Whales, church, Girl Scout cookies, Jerry's Kids, cancer drives, the mission, etc. etc. etc. and totaled that we gave five percent of our income. Surely that would be enough.

How much grain did Musa's family need, anyway?

What a test of faith it was to commit to giving ten percent.

Every promise I had heard about it came true. The more we gave, the more we got in return. Proverbs says, "One man gives freely yet grows all the richer; another withholds what he should give and only suffers want."

My daddy, the farmer, was right. "I shovel what I have to God, and He shovels back, but His shovel is bigger than mine."

Years later I read about a rich man with the same philosophy. William Volker, the inventor of the roll-up window shade, was quite young when he amassed his fortune. He kept one million dollars and gave all the rest away. His friends thought he was nuts! One admitted, "I was sure you'd end up a pauper, but you're richer than ever, despite all the money you've shoveled out over all the years."

Warren Buffett gave away about eighty-five percent of his $44 billion fortune to charity. The largest portion—five-sixths—went to the Bill and Melinda Gates Foundation. The money will be used to seek cures for the world's worst diseases and to improve American education. "There is no reason we can't cure the top twenty diseases," Gates said.

Volker answered, "God has a bigger shovel."

Daddy wasn't just talking about seed corn.

Gordon Groth, former president of Electra manufacturing, said he knew of regular churchgoers who quit attending services but did not quit tithing once they had stopped coming

> *"This is what we are all about. We plant the seeds that one day will grow. We water seeds already planted, knowing they hold future promise. We lay foundations that will need further development. We provide yeast that produces effects far beyond our capabilities. We cannot do everything, and there is a sense of liberation in realizing that. This enables us to do something and do it very well. It may be incomplete, but it is a beginning, a step along the way, an opportunity for the Lord's grace to enter and do the rest."*
> —*Archbishop Oscar Romero*

because they were afraid their material blessings would disappear if they did!

Many employers encourage their staff to tithe and/or do community service. They know it not only benefits the community, but also the employee. Giving makes people feel powerful, and employers are attracted to that. The end result is increased success for the employee and the employer.

How did you feel the last time you gave of your money or service? You projected those feelings, and others noticed. Everyone won.

Tithing includes donations made not only via religious institutions, but all contributions to all causes. And tithing isn't only giving of our treasures but giving of our time and talents. We can give by teaching someone to read, shoveling a neighbor's sidewalk, phoning a shut-in, or sending a get-well card. No effort is too small.

As we strive to find this balance of involvement, it helps to realize we do not have to do it all.

Remember the Bible story of the little boy who donated his few loaves of bread and fishes and Jesus turned them into enough food to feed thousands? Notice that He did not ask the boy to organize the fishermen or create unions for bread bakers. He asked him to give what he had.

Like us.

I was right when, as a kid trick or treating for UNICEF, I determined we are called to be our brothers' keepers. We can all make a difference.

Traditional Jews believe that when we leave this world it ought to be a better place than when we entered it. The concept is known as *Tikkun Olam*, which means, "Repair of the World"—or, in other words, *making the world a better place for all living things.*

There are over 1,100,000 nonprofit organizations in the United States alone. How marvelous that we gather as citizens, using the power of our freedom, to serve others. Still, the needs can seem overwhelming. Confronted by that, we ponder how miniscule our contributions are in the scope of things, and we wonder, is my small part really worth it?

"Do unto others as you would have them do unto you."
—Christianity

"Hurt not others in ways that you yourself would find hurtful."
—Buddhism

"What is hateful to you, do not to your fellow man."
—Judaism

"No one of you is a believer until he desires for his brother that which he desires for himself."
—Islam

"Blessed is he who preferred his brother before himself."
—Baba'i Faith

"Do not do to others what you would not have them do to you."
—Confucianism

Indeed it is! Remember, no effort is too small. Everything you do matters far more than you know and has ramifications far beyond your knowledge or expectations. You may not be called to rescue babies in cardboard boxes in a third world country, but you rescue people every day by serving.

Mother Teresa, my hero, said it best: "I cannot do great things. I can only do small things, with great love."

Like you.

Chapter Twelve

Finding Peace in Your "War Zone"

Creating Peace in Our Lives

A cool, gentle breeze blew my hair across my sweaty cheek as the open-air bus transported us to the motel. Palm trees and colorful flowers provided a peaceful setting.

But I didn't feel at peace.

Days of caring for all the infants had distracted my fear, but now, in this lull, it resurfaced, too powerful to suppress: *How long will it take to check all the babies? How long will we have to stay here? I won't feel safe again until I'm on US soil.*

The bus dropped us off at the motel, and Ross and I sauntered past a bed of lush, exquisite flowers amidst swaying palm trees. I inhaled the fresh, sweet air, trying to breathe in the tranquility.

It was no use.

I blurted out, "I know I'm paranoid, Ross, but I still don't feel safe here." Ashamed of my stubborn fear, I went on. "It's suspected that the Vietcong shot down one planeload of orphans. What if they try to bomb these babies here?"

He listened with a straight face. "LeAnn, no country would bomb a US air base as powerful as this."

"I suppose not," I heard myself say.

He patted my back gently. "We're safe here. Really."

"Of course," I said with fake confidence.

I entered our room and plopped onto the floral bedspread while Carol took a shower. The fluffy pillow under my head reminded me that I'd left my sweater at the center. I hoped one of the workers would wear it and remember me.

Ross's words echoed in my head: "We're safe here."

Yet the peace I craved eluded me.

After a long warm bath, Carol and I met Ross and Sister Terese at the mess hall. The American cuisine tasted great.

I declined the salad.

We ate together, slowly, quietly. We welcomed the relaxation but admitted to each other an uncomfortable sense of loss and emptiness.

Sister Terese knew the cure. "Let's go see the babies!" she declared.

"And find my son!"

Instantly, we took our trays to the conveyor belt and rushed to the gymnasium, which appeared to be the size of a hanger. Hundreds of single-bed mattresses lay in neat rows, covered with white sheets, with diapers, clothes, and toys stacked on one end. We beamed to see our babies, each with their own bed and caregiver. The many unoccupied mattresses awaited the arrival of more children.

Sister Terese burst into tears. "Somebody cares for them," she said, blowing her nose and wiping her eyes. "Somebody besides us cares for them."

After a group hug, I couldn't wait another minute, and we split up to find Mitch.

Nagging fear crept over me as I imagined that somehow he could have been lost. Still amazed by the maternal instinct that bonded me to him, I marched slowly between the rows, rhythmically moving my head from left to right, staring at each baby.

Then, there he was.

In the middle of the gym I found him sitting contently in the arms of a volunteer.

"He's my son," I told the curly-haired woman who looked at me skeptically.

As if to prove it, Mitchell reached for me. Having him back in my arms made me feel complete.

"You're a lucky mama," the woman said. "He is a wonderful baby. The doctor was just here and said he's a healthy one, too."

Relieved, I swayed him back and forth in my arms.

Ross, Carol, and Sister joined me, and we all listened as the Air Force wives told us how two of our babies had been hospitalized but were expected to do very well. Dehydration and fever were the primary problems, and these wee ones had no reserve.

My friends went back to the motel, but I couldn't leave Mitch. Not yet. We played on the mattress for a while, peek-a-booing and rolling a little ball back and forth. When the lights in the gymnasium dimmed, I sat cross-legged, rocking him in my arms. He nestled his head into my neck and breathed softly as I sang him our family's favorite lullabies.

Soon he was asleep, and I gently laid him on his tummy and covered him with a light blanket. I kissed his soft, smooth cheek. "Good night, son." I loved how that sounded.

Lightheaded and weak, I headed back to my room. I donned my pajamas, turned out the light, and collapsed into bed. My innards roared so loudly, Carol and I giggled with each rumble.

It felt good to laugh again. Then we settled down, and I lay in the quiet darkness. I silently prayed in thanksgiving for our son.

For our safety.

Finally, a feeling of calm tranquility enveloped me—one I had not known since the day the plane had crashed. Tears of relief and joy trickled onto my crisp pillowcase.

Peace at last.

■ ■ ■

We cannot create a world of peace until we create it within ourselves.

Are there non-peaceful situations in your home? community? work?
the world?

Think about the people involved in the conflict. Would you agree that those people lack peace within? People who are grumpy, addicted, or abusive bring that to their families, to their work, to your traffic, and our world.

Now examine the non-peaceful circumstances in your personal life. Are those not areas where you lack peace?

Mahatma Gandhi said, "We must become the change we seek in the world."

You have the power to create peace in your life.

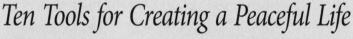

Ten Tools for Creating a Peaceful Life

1) Take Control

Repeat and live the serenity prayer: God, grant me the serenity to accept the things I cannot change, the courage to change the things I can, and the wisdom to know the difference. *Who is the boss of you? Who says how much you eat, how much you sleep, how much you buy, how much you cry, how much you play, how much you pray? You do. Take control. It's your decision.*

2) Simplify
De-clutter. Downsize. Right-size. Slow down. What material goods can you let go of? What time-takers can you release? What activities can you cease? What demands can you delegate? You can you simplify your life. It's your decision.

3) Respect Yourself and Others
Be your own best friend. Take care of yourself. How will you make time to eat, sleep, exercise, breathe, relax, think positive, forgive, laugh, pray? Listen carefully to others, especially those who disagree with you. Trust that their opinions are rooted as deeply in their moral convictions as yours. How will you treat them as you want to be treated? Everything can be spoken in kindness. Everything. It's your decision.

4) Do Goodwill
You make a living by what you get; you make a life by what you give.How will you serve others in a balanced way? It's your decision.

5) Choose Calm
Forego a manic way of life. How will you turn off the noise? Where will you seek quiet? Connect with nature. Breathe and relax.Calm is trust in action. Trust. Be calm. It's your decision.

6) Redefine Success
Life is a series of transitions. Step back and re-evaluate your course. If you were going to die tomorrow, what would you regret not doing today? Is there a personal price you are paying for trying to have or do too much? Are you leaving a legacy of good? Are you living your priorities? Your success is your decision.

7) Decide to Be Happy
Create the life you want to live. What do you want more of? Less of? Don't be so busy saving the world that you forget to savor it. Happiness is a choice. It's your decision.

8) Be Grateful

The acknowledgement of past blessings activates new ones. At the end of every day, list five things you are grateful for. Write letters of gratitude to ten people who have helped you in life. Be grateful for the privilege of living, and your life will grow increasingly happier. It's your decision.

9) Have Faith

Believe in a Power bigger than you. Connect with your Creator. Trust. Hope. Let go. Let God.

10) Live Your Priorities.

Commit to devoting your time and love to the priorities in your life. As you pour yourself into them, they will fill you. Are you living your priorities? It's your decision.

You must create inner peace. The peace of the world is depending on it.

By balancing your life physically, mentally, and spiritually, you will become whole and happy. With this, you will create peace at the center of your life. You will let go of anxiety and fear and find the courage and confidence to handle your problems and live a life of great joy and less stress.

You'll find peace in your "war zones."

Chapter Thirteen

Rolling on the Floor in Joy!

Living a Joy-Filled Life

"I've never seen so many lights or so much activity here," the pilot announced as we circled the airport in Iowa. "There must be a celebrity on this flight."

I turned around, trying to look nonchalant as I gazed at the passengers and wondered who that might be. I didn't recognize anyone famous.

When the plane landed and came to a stop, my heart thumped rapidly as I stood with Mitchell in my arms. The attendant reminded me that it was cool in Cedar Rapids and gave me a blue flight blanket to put around him.

I descended the stairs, and, when my feet touched the runway, I was tempted to sprint into the building and Mark's arms. When I'd called him from our layover in Hawaii, I had my speech rehearsed to tell him about Mitch. But before I could speak, he said through tears, "Just tell me you have our son."

It took all the restraint I could muster to walk slowly into the building. But I couldn't see. Bright lights glared in my eyes. Confused, I stopped for a moment to try to grasp what was happening. Cameras flashed. Reporters shouted questions.

I inched my way forward through the blinding glare. Mark stepped through the lights with open arms, his smile shining across his face.

I eased into his embrace and held tight.

More than once in Saigon, I had feared I would never again feel this touch. I couldn't let go as I felt his arms wrapping around me and our son.

The joy was overwhelming.

This was all I needed in the world.

My life was complete.

I stepped back so Mark could see Mitchell, who opened his arms and reached for his daddy. Mark's eyes brimmed with tears as he drew him to his heart.

Past him, I saw my mom and sisters, Mary and Theresa, there to support me, just as they had done all my life. Having anticipated this media madness, my sister Diane stayed home with our daughters. I felt confused, like I was dreaming when I hugged them and other relatives who had come to meet the plane.

My mind was a whirlwind.

Mark seemed to be directing me down a corridor away from the crowds and press.

"You're going to have to trust me on this one, honey," he said. "You're going to hold a press conference."

I couldn't believe my ears.

"Mark, I can't. I don't want to. I only want to go home."

"You have no idea what's been going on here since you've been gone. The newspapers and TV reporters have been calling day and night. This is the biggest story that's happened in a long time. They all promised that if you talk to them now, they'll leave us alone."

By that time we were entering a large room filled with reporters. Microphones cluttered the long table in front.

Everything was happening so fast.

I wanted desperately to turn and leave but trusted Mark absolutely.

I stifled a laugh as I sat down in front of all those mikes and all those people. It seemed like something you would see on *Meet the Press*, not something I should be doing. Mark and I took turns holding Mitchell as the questions were fired at us. Mitchell smiled and patted his hands and waved at the lights.

Finally, Mark said that was enough and ended the session. Still, persistent reporters called out questions and attempted to follow us to the parking lot. Mark turned and reminded them firmly of the deal that had been promised, and they retreated as we made our way to the car.

"I can't wait to go home with you," I said softly as I hugged Mark again before getting in.

"We're not going home," he apologized. He knew I'd be disappointed. "We're going to your mom's."

He explained the badgering he had experienced from the reporters the past few days. He didn't trust them to honor the agreement to respect our privacy.

I was indeed disappointed. This was not at all how I had envisioned our homecoming. Yet going to mom's, where I'd be pampered and nurtured and surrounded by my big loving family, did sound appealing.

During the thirty-minute ride to Vinton, alone with Mark and Mitchell, I felt carefree. There was so much we both wanted to say, but we hardly knew where to begin. Mostly, I just wanted to hear all about him and the girls. No one had told Angela and Christie about my bringing Mitchell home. He thought it would be wonderful to tell them in person because they loved "surprises." I knew they'd be asleep at Diane's since it was nearly midnight, but I wanted to go just to see them, not wake them.

Until I entered mom's house.

Something inside me clicked off. The stress that had provided the energy to keep going was suddenly gone. Exhaustion immobilized me. It didn't take much to convince me that I should wait until morning to see our girls.

We made Mitchell a mattress of blankets on the floor next to our bed in the guest room. Mom apologized for the poor accommodations for him on short notice. I laughed as I tried to explain how he slept on mats on floors throughout this trip and began to tell them about the center in Saigon with scores of babies.

A part of me wanted to stay up all night and talk endlessly about all that had happened. I knew they would have listened if my fatigue had not made it impossible.

After hugging Mom and thanking her for being there for us, I shut off the light and slipped into bed with Mark. I felt the strong, safe embrace of love I had longed for so often in the past ten days. It was then that the tears I had suppressed throughout this incredible day poured out.

I was up several times in the night with stomachaches and diarrhea but still managed to sleep until the late hour of 9:00 when I heard Angela and Christie's voices. I snuck out of bed, tiptoed past Mitchell, and rushed to the living room.

"Hi, Mommy!" Angela and Christie chimed as their pigtails bobbed. I stooped to hug them both at the same time. I laughed to keep from crying as they bounced into my arms. I pretended to fall backward onto the floor as they smothered me with kisses. How wonderful to feel their chubby little arms around me as we rolled on the floor in joy!

Then, there he was.

Mitch had crawled from the bedroom to the doorway. Before I could speak any words of explanation, he crept into my lap with the girls. They gasped.

Angela beamed at me and said, "This must be my brother!"

■ ■ ■

Someone once said happiness is a choice. Although that is likely oversimplified, it is still true. You have the power to choose and to create a happy life. Don't put happiness on hold. The time to enjoy your life is now. It takes as much effort to live an unrewarding life as it does to lead a rewarding, joy-filled one. It depends on your choices.

The life lessons I've shared in this book are basic. The tools are simple (though not always easy!). Deep down, do you believe them?

Then, do them.

Take one chapter at a time…or begin applying the principles simultaneously. Keep the book on your nightstand as a reference.

Invite a friend or form a group to enjoy the journey together.

Share the book and your efforts with others.

Ask for your "juice" and their support. Then, watch the positive results unfold.

You *can* balance your life physically, mentally, and spiritually, you *can* make healthy good decisions, you *can* truly live your priorities, and when you do, you are in a better place to make an even bigger difference in this world.

Gandhi said, "We must become the change we seek in the world."

Change.

You can do this.

You deserve it.

Now, embrace all you love and, with peace in your heart, go roll on the floor in joy!

— The End —

More Books by LeAnn

This Must Be My Brother

Adrift in the Storms

Chicken Soup for the Nurse's Soul

Chicken Soup for the Christian Woman's Soul

Chicken Soup for the Caregiver's Soul

Chicken Soup for the Father and Daughter Soul

Chicken Soup for the Grandma's Soul

Chicken Soup for the Mother and Son Soul

Chicken Soup for the Christian Soul 2

Chicken Soup for the Nurse's Soul, Second Dose

Chicken Soup for the Adopted Soul

Chicken Soup for the Catholic Soul

About the Author

LeAnn Thieman is a nationally acclaimed professional speaker, author, and nurse who was "accidentally" caught up in the Vietnam Orphan Airlift in 1975. Her book *This Must Be My Brother* details her daring adventure of helping to rescue three hundred babies as Saigon was falling to the Communists. An ordinary person, she struggled through extraordinary circumstances and found the courage to succeed. LeAnn has been featured in *Newsweek Magazine's Voices of the Century* issue, FOX-TV, BBC, NPR, PBS, PAX-TV's *It's a Miracle*, and countless radio and TV programs.

As a renowned motivational speaker, she shares life-changing lessons learned from her airlift and nursing experiences. Believing we all have individual "war zones," LeAnn inspires audiences to balance their lives, truly live their priorities, and make a difference in the world. An expert in nurse recruitment and retention, she helps organizations hire and inspire their nurses and care-giving team members.

LeAnn is one of about ten percent of speakers worldwide to have earned the Certified Speaking Professional Designation.

She and Mark, her husband of thirty-seven years, reside in Colorado, where they enjoy their "empty nest." Their two daughters, Angela and Christie, and son Mitch have "flown the coop" but are still drawn under their mother's wing when she needs them!